AF538900

Biological Weapons

Issues and Threats

Editors

P.R.Chari

Arpit Rajain

Institute of Peace and Conflict Studies
New Delhi

India Research Press
New Delhi

India Research Press
B-4/22, Safdarjung Enclave,
New Delhi – 110 029.
Ph.: 24694610; Fax : 24618637
bahrisons@vsnl.com
www.indiaresearchpress.com
contact@indiaresearchpress.com

ISBN : 81-88353-18-3

Cataloguing in Publication Data
P. R. Chari, Arpit Rajain
Biological Weapons Issues and Threats
Editors : P. R. Chari, Arpit Rajain

Includes bibliographical references and index.

1. Bilogical Weapons 2. South Asia Security 3. Biological Warfare
I. Title II. Author

ISBN : 81-88353-18-3

Printed in India at Focus Impressions, New Delhi – 110 003.

PREFACE

The deliberate use of disease to prosecute war is as old as history itself. War is a cruel enterprise with victory as its ultimate, unequivocal goal; hence rules devised to circumscribe these means for humanitarian and other laudable purposes cannot be pursued beyond a point. Do weapons of mass destruction (WMD) make a difference to such modes of thinking? The easy reference to nuclear weapons during the recent inter-state crises witnessed in the South Asian region would question the belief that nuclear weapons, the prime WMD, has made a seminal difference to the holding out of threats and taking provocative actions that could lead to conflict.

Bacteriological warfare and the use of biological agents and toxins to cause mass deaths are not new. What is new is two factors at the present time that have made the threat of (bacteriological) biological agents and toxins more salient and significant.

- First, rapid advances in molecular biology and genetic engineering during the 1980s has made possible the use of manipulative techniques to develop altogether new types of disease—causing bacteria and virus that could be resistant to known vaccines. A case in point is recent research in Australia to insert the interleukin-4 gene, which controls immune responses, into the mouse pox virus. This has made it deadly for naturally immune mice and even for vaccinated mice. The possibility of researchers developing deadly diseases using these techniques no longer lies in the realm of fantasy and science fiction, but can be converted into cold reality.
- Second, national security establishments, influenced by the history of biowarfare have largely focused on its use by states against their adversaries. For several reasons that need not detain us, it is unlikely, though not impossible, for states to attack each other with biological weapons in future. The ease of deniability makes possible the use of biowarfare by states, especially by the weak against the strong, since the onset of disease symptoms takes time to manifest itself. But the greater likelihood of biological weapons becoming the instruments of choice for terrorists should be a matter of immediate concern. 9/11 in 2001 and the sarin attack

in the Tokyo subway (1995) established two dubious norms, viz. the usability of innovative WMDs (commercial aircraft) to serve terrorist purposes, and the possibility of chemical and biological weapons becoming the instruments to serve their ends.

These two factors emphasise the need for the international community to protect itself against biological weapons and toxins, which urgently requires a change in the mindset of security establishments around the world; they are traditionally inclined towards focusing their attention on nuclear weapons in the WMD pantheon to the near exclusion of chemical and biological weapons. Some part of this insouciance is understandable because defence against biological weapons is difficult and must include, besides military countermeasures, public health measures—preventive and curative—that are low key and uncertain of success; hence they have not commanded the same attention as defending against either a conventional or nuclear attack. Biological warfare has a naturally low profile.

The Geneva Protocol for the Prohibition of the Use in War of Asphyxiating, Poisonous or Other Gases and of Bacteriological Methods of Warfare (1925) had consolidated the earlier prohibitions against the use of poisonous gases declared at the International Peace Conferences (1899 and 1907) held in The Hague and reiterated in the Treaty of Versailles (1919); the Geneva Protocol added a ban on bacteriological weapons. However, although it banned the use of bacteriological weapons in conflict, the Geneva Protocol did not prohibit the development, production, stockpiling or otherwise acquiring or retaining these weapons. Article I of the Convention on the Prohibition of the Development, Production and Stockpiling of Bacteriological (Biological) and Toxin Weapons and on Their Destruction (1972) addresses these shortcomings.

Unfortunately, the BTWC has no provisions for its verification and therefore offends the salubrious principle "Trust but Verify" enunciated by a former American President. Whether signatories to the BTWC are in compliance with its provisions largely remains a matter of trust; disconcertingly, many of the State Parties are known to possess stockpiles of biological weapons This has greatly eroded the value of the Convention as a measure of arms control to eradicate an entire class of weapons of mass destruction. The possibility of State Parties making available their stocks of biological weapons to *sub rosa* organisations, either deliberately or due to lack of adequate control over their ssockpiles, is no longer an abstract question. The BTWC regime, indeed, is under imminent danger from "the hazards of violations, evasions and bio-terrorism".

Cognizant of these limitations in the BTWC and conscious of the need to provide for verification arrangements to ensure its credibility, the State Parties have been negotiating a Verification Protocol for much of the last decade. This task was not easy because various interests had to be balanced against each other: the requirements of international security had to be weighed against national sovereignty, the need for transparency had to be balanced against that of secrecy for commercial reasons and so on. There is also the conundrum of how to accommodate advances in science due to new and emerging technologies within the BTWC, as this would make identification of prohibited biological agents and toxins much more problematical. The essays in this volume address some of these difficult issues like the natural anxieties in the biotech industry about the verification regime compromising legitimate commercial secrecy, and the manner in which the verification arrangements established for the Chemical Weapons Convention are comparable with those contemplated for the BTWC. The need for States to enact domestic legislation to implement the BTWC is another issue of significance for its verification. At the military security level two essays explore the future dangers of bioterrorism and the threat posed by biological weapons as also the defence possible against them.

At the end of six years of hard negotiations two draft texts for the Verification Protocol became available by the middle of 2001. It is ironical that the United States at this critical juncture, when the need for a Verification Protocol is the greatest, has chosen to torpedo these efforts by suggesting that the body to negotiate the Verification Protocol should be scrapped and these negotiations suspended, without any clear vision of what verification arrangements might be emplaced instead. In fact, the United States desires that these negotiations should be postponed till 2006. The contours of the likely endgame in Geneva has also been speculated upon in one of the essays. As expected the Review Conference was reconvened in November 2002. By way of a retrospective analysis, two case studies have also been added to this volume. They deal with the plague epidemic in Surat (1994) and Himachal Pradesh (2002) that have found a place in the relevant literature, and the anthrax mail attacks in the Unitad States following 9/11 that have grave implications for national and international security.

It is hoped that these essays will go some way towards illuminating the issues governing the establishment of a verification regime for the BTWC, and enlarging the understanding on India's position on the various issues embedded in that regime.

March 2003 P. R. Chari

CONTENTS

Acknowledgements

This book would not have been possible without the support of several people who contributed to the project academically and in other ways. We are especially thankful to all those who participated in the preparatory conference held on 9 October 2002 at the India Habitat Centre to discuss the draft papers that have been presented in this volume. Particular mention must be made of Dr. R.V. Swamy, Mr. A. K. Verma, Air Chief Marshal S. K. Mehra, Brigadier Subhash Kapila, Dr. Sandhya Tiwari and several serving armed forces officials from the Army, Navy and the Air Force.

We would like to gratefully acknowledge the grant received from the Ministry of External Affairs that funded the conference. We are particularly grateful to Joint Secretary (D&ISA) Dr. S. K. Sharma for his cooperation and participation in the successful completion of this project. Needless to add, the MEA is not responsible for either the facts or the conclusions drawn herein by the respective authors in the various essays published in this book.

We would also like to thank the research staff at the IPCS, particularly Divya Srivastava and Vivek Shankar Mathur, for their unstinting support. As always, the support staff at the Institute, S. L. Vermani, Sapna, Vijay and Surinder took care of the administrative arrangements and competently handled the unforeseen hitches.

CWC and BTWC: Lessons from the Verification Process

Arpit Rajain

Following the successful negotiation of the Chemical Weapons Convention (CWC) at the Conference on Disarmament, Geneva and its opening for signature a wave of optimism permeated the arms control community. The CWC was seen as a case study for arms control and disarmament approaches in the future.[1] It was the first multilateral treaty designed to destroy an entire class of weapons of mass destruction with the most comprehensive verification system yet designed for a multilateral disarmament treaty. The arms control community now felt that there were good prospects for concluding new arms control treaties and for improving existing treaties, including the Biological Weapons Convention (BWC), which would incorporate the CWC's comprehensive and stringent verification regime.

At the beginning of this new millennium, interest and concern about proliferation seems to be wavering, creating uncertainty about the international community's commitment to non-proliferation. The message so far seems to signify a shift away from multilateralism. Instead of strengthening their respective regimes, what is being revealed is the hollowness of commitments made by states today. Non-proliferation rhetoric is not being supported by deployment of resources or political will.

At the heart of the chem-bio arms control regime are the CWC and the BTWC which are in turn premised on the 1927 Geneva Protocol. On the face of it the two treaties, the CWC and the BTWC seem to have much in common, but a closer scrutiny reveals that it is not so. Under the BTWC, all biological and toxin warfare agents, munitions and delivery systems were to have been destroyed or diverted to peaceful purposes within

---

1. Letts, M., Mathews, R. J., McCormack, T.L. and Moraitis, C., "The Conclusion of the Chemical Weapons Convention: An Australian Perspective", *Arms Control*, Vol. 14, No. 3 (December 1993), pp. 311–32.

nine months after the treaty's entry into force on 26 March 1975. Countries that acceded to the CWC, on the contrary had to eliminate their existing stockpiles, if any, within 10 years, with the possibility of a five year extension in exceptional cases.

The Biological and Chemical Threat

Against the backdrop of the Anthrax attacks post 9/11 and the attempts by various non-state actors to acquire biological and chemical weapons, the prospect of the proliferation of biological and chemical weapons took on alarming dimensions. Perhaps the most daunting challenge for intelligence analysts comes from biological and chemical weapons. Some trends highlight this:

First, given the level of motivation, resources and organisation exhibited by the Al Qaeda during the attack on the WTC, the threat from the non-state actors cannot be underestimated. Much of the earlier literature seemed to highlight the technological difficulties that any non-state actor is likely to face in assembling these weapons. But the Aum Shinrikyo and the Al Qaeda have shattered such notions. The threat is there in breadth and sophistication.

Second, while new alliances are being formed and old ones are being renewed the world is preparing to fight a new unseen, stateless enemy. But these regime structures have suffered a setback with the US moving away from the multilateral process to strengthen the BWC.

Third, in spite of the surge in intelligence gathering there remain huge gaps between the known and the unknown. The enemy will always retain the element of surprise. Many states like Iran, Iraq, Libya, North Korea, and Syria are pursuing offensive chem-bio warfare programmes and non-state actors continue in their bid to gather whatever weapons of mass destruction they can acquire.[2] Groups like Al Qaeda have international networks and outreach, which adds to uncertainty. Non-state actors operate with much less legal and political constraints than states.

---

2. The states of concern in the Statement by George J. Tenet, Director of Central Intelligence Before the Senate Foreign Relations Committee on "The Worldwide Threat in 2000: Global Realities of Our National Security", 21 March 2000, available at the database of the Centre for Non-Proliferation Studies, at http://www.cns.miis.edu, accessed on 17 August 2002.

Fourth, unlike conventional weapons, chem-bio weapons can be directed against crops and livestock with lethal effect. Plant and animal pathogens may be used against agricultural targets, causing both economic devastation, and the possibility that a criminal group might seek to exploit such an attack for economic advantage.

Fifth, apart from non-state actor some states could perceive chem-bio weapons as the 'poor man's nuke's This increases the likelihood of chemo-bio weapons being used in insurgencies and for tactical applications in regional conflicts, increasing the probability that such conflicts will be deadly and destabilising.

Sixth, CBW agents could potentially become more lethal with the advances in science and biotechnology. This leads to the prospect of a new array of toxins or live agents that require new detection methods, preventative measures, and treatment. And on the chemical side, there is a growing risk that new and difficult-to-combat agents will become available to hostile countries or sub-national groups.

Seventh, CBW programmes are becoming and will continue to become more self-sufficient, thereby challenging detection and deterrence efforts, and limiting interdiction opportunities. There continues to be a genuine overlap between legitimate research and commercial biotechnology and offensive warfare programmes. This dual-use capability lends itself to conduct clandestine CBW research and rapid agent and toxin production.

Eighth, progress in science has helped in acquiring innovative dissemination techniques, delivery options, and strategies for CBW use. There is a concern in the intelligence community about state and non-state actors acquiring advanced technologies to design, test, and produce highly effective munitions and sophisticated delivery systems.

Verification

The CWC contains an ambitious verification regime envisaging comprehensive data reporting and detailed on-site inspections. All State Party's facilities that produce or consume treaty-limited "scheduled" chemicals above certain levels or thresholds are obliged to report those activities under the CWC.

Any facilities that meet specified production or consumption thresholds found in the CWC must be "declared" by the State Party and become subject to routine inspections. They consist of an initial inspection and periodic follow-ups, called systematic or routine inspections. The purpose of routine inspections is to verify, through on-site inspection, each State Party's declared chemical activities. The Technical Secretariat of the CWC's organisation for the Prohibition of Chemical Weapons (OPCW) reviews data declarations and conducts on-site inspections using multinational inspection teams employed by the organisation.

Concerns about compliance with the Convention, including those not resolved during routine inspections, can be addressed through challenge inspections. Conducted by the OPCW, a challenge inspection may be requested by any CWC State Party at any facility believed to be conducting prohibited CW activities. State Parties to the CWC do not have the right to refuse a challenge inspection. No challenge inspections, however, have been initiated to date. The first challenge inspection is long overdue, as conducting a challenge inspection would put all other States Parties on notice that CWC non-compliance would not be tolerated, and this would invigorate the deterrent value of the verification regime.[3]

The CWC-verification system has several components. Some are inspection activities of various types. These are the "verification measures provided for in this Convention" which the OPCW Technical Secretariat, according to CWC Article VIII.37, must carry out.[4] More specifically, according to the CWC Verification Annex Part II.3, these activities are to be performed by the Secretariat's "designated inspectors and inspection assistants", and only by them.[5] Article IX of the CWC and Part X of the Verification Annex specifically details the verification system remain the declaration activities: collection, reporting and processing of specified kinds of information that relate to chemical weapons or to technologies that could be used to make them. Herein lies a division of labour that underpins the entire verification regime. The National Authorities are responsible for collecting and reporting the information that the

3. Jonathan B. Tucker (ed), *The Conduct of Challenge Inspections under the Chemical Weapons Convention*, Proceedings of an Expert Workshop, 29-31 May 2002, Washington DC (Washington DC: Monterey Institute of International Studies, 2002)

4. See Text of Convention on the Prohibition of the Development, Production, Stockpiling and use of Chemical Weapons and on their Destruction, available at http://www.opcw.org.

5. *Ibid.*

Convention obliges States Parties to declare either at regular intervals or when occasion arises, depending on the type of information involved. The Technical Secretariat is responsible for receiving and processing the declarations and, through 'routine inspection' procedures, for validating some of them. To be able to make the declarations, the National Authorities must have entered into an intimate monitoring relationship with all the relevant parts of their countries' technological base, including civil industry. High standards of monitoring are, in principle, assured through mutual scrutiny of the National Authorities and the Technical Secretariat instituted by the international procedures prescribed under the treaty. The possibility of a short-notice challenge inspection at virtually any location is a modality also prescribed by the Convention to deter possible infractions.

Reporting of Unusual Outbreaks of Disease

The Ad Hoc Group (AHG), until calls began for winding it up, was considering measures to strengthen the Biological and Toxin Weapons Convention (BTWC) through a legally binding, universally acceptable, verification protocol. It is evident that the implementation of a legally binding instrument will require States Parties to take appropriate national measures. Consequently, Article X relating to National Implementation Measures in the Draft Protocol is of vital importance in ensuring that it achieves its objective of strengthening the BTWC.

Declarations and Visits

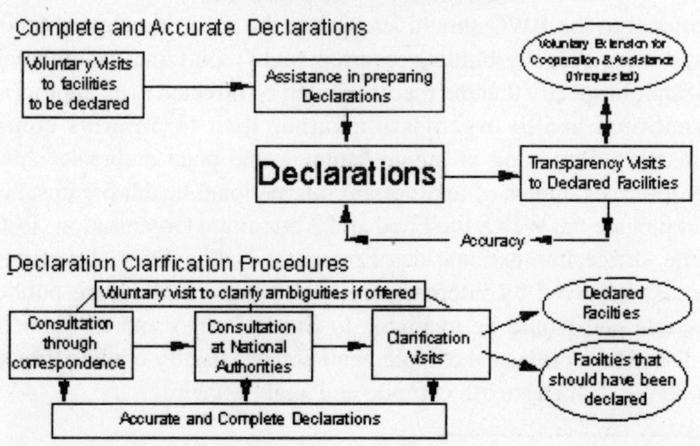

*Graham S. Pearson and Malcolm R. Dando, Visits: An Essential and Effective Pillar, University of Bradford, Briefing Paper No. 18, January 1999. Available on http://www.brad.ac.uk/acad/sbtwc

Unusual outbreaks of disease most often have natural causes, despite their unusual attributes. However, because such outbreaks could also result from the use or release of biological weapons agents, and because even natural outbreaks might provoke suspicions of non-compliance, States Parties to the BWC have agreed that information on unusual outbreaks should be exchanged as a confidence-building measure. However, experience with this confidence-building measure makes it clear that States Parties are reluctant to report outbreaks in connection with the BWC, even when they have willingly reported them to the World Health Organisation (WHO).

In the AHG there has been considerable debate about natural outbreaks of disease when the Non-Aligned and some other countries presented a working paper in January 1998 suggesting the exclusion of all natural outbreaks of disease from investigations under the Protocol.[6] This paper states "the investigation, diagnosis, treatment, and control of disease fall primarily within the domain of the public healthcare system of each country...Investigation and control of disease remains its sovereign responsibility, even if that country were to seek international assistance... all natural outbreaks of disease fall in the domain of public health and do not pose a compliance concern to the Biological and Toxin Weapons Convention (BTWC) and are therefore of no concern to the Convention".[7]

A Protocol to the BWC should strengthen the reporting expectation by incorporating a legally-binding requirement to report unusual outbreaks, and it should specify that the reports should be directed to an appropriate international health organisation rather than to an arms control organisation. Reporting of human, animal, and plant outbreaks should be required; examples of appropriate international health organisations would include the WHO, the Food and Agriculture Organisation (FAO), and the Office International des Épizooties (OIE). Official reports of outbreaks received by international health organisations are publicly accessible and would be available to States Parties and to the office established to coordinate the implementation of a legally-binding Protocol to the BWC, which should compile and analyse them.

---

6. Group of NAM and other countries, Investigations: Exclusion of All Natural Outbreaks of Disease, BWC/AD HOC/GROUP/WP.262, 23 January 1998.
7. *Ibid.* India was a party to this Working Paper.

With the CWC negotiations having reached their logical conclusion, it was suggested that there are lessons from the negotiation of the CWC that might be of use to the negotiation of a Protocol for the BWC. This brings up the question, in the light of the current status of the BWC Protocol negotiations, if any of the lessons from the CWC "end-game" are applicable to the "end-game" negotiations of the BWC Protocol. It is essential to note that in terms of a way ahead for the BWC Protocol, which is currently in abeyance, it would be useful to go back to 1988, when people started thinking the CWC could be concluded within 12 months, after which the atmosphere in the CWC negotiations became more serious. Participants started to undertake a range of activities in capitals, including surveys of industry, practice inspections, and outreach to chemical industry. It is also useful to consider proposals suggested by Australia in 1991 to conclude the CWC negotiations during 1992. These included:

- greater involvement of capital-based officials in the negotiations;
- movement away from the multiple Working Groups towards a "less formalistic" structure in the negotiations;
- greater use of private consultations via a system of Friends of the Chair so as to "allow for compromises to emerge without having to be publicly viewed and without negotiators being seen as gaining or losing face";
- a meeting of the Ad Hoc Committee at ministerial level;
- more regional dialogue; and
- a meeting of the prospective or acting heads of national implementation authorities.
- This would suggest an increase in capital-based activities that might add greater interest and momentum to the negotiation process in Geneva, which, in turn, might benefit from a "less formalistic" negotiation process in the AHG.

Apart from the cultural aspect of these negotiations there are various parameters along which the two treaties can be compared.

Comparison of the BTWC and its Protocol Regime with that of the CWC:[8]

8. Adapted from written testimony of Professor Graham S. Pearson, To The Subcommittee on National Security, Veteran Affairs and International Relations of The Committee on Government Reform, Washington, DC, 10 July 2001, available at http://.www.fas.org/bwc/news/peartest.htm, accessed on 12 October 2001.

BTWC and its Protocol Regime	CWC Regime
Mandatory declarations -- range of facilities (BL-4, BL-3*, work with listed agents*, production, …) -- requires declaration of biological defence -- measures to ensure submission	Mandatory declarations --focussed on chemical production facilities --no declarations yet of chemical defence --no measures to ensure submission
Declaration follow-up procedures -- explicit and structured -- analysis of declarations --randomly-selected transparency visits	Declaration follow-up procedures --implicit and unstructured -- routine inspections of production facilities for scheduled chemicals and DOCs (discrete organic chemicals)
Declaration clarification procedures -- clarification visits	No declaration clarification procedures -- implicit not elaborate
Voluntary assistance visits	No provision for voluntary assistance visits -- implicit not elaborated
Non-compliance concerns -- Consultations >>> Investigations	Non-compliance concerns -- Consultations >>> Investigations
Field investigation -- includes investigation of releases	Investigation of alleged use -- no investigation of other releases
Facility investigation -- team size and duration limited	Challenge inspection -- duration limited
Transfer procedures	Transfer controls
Assistance -- provisions similar to CWC	Assistance
International Cooperation -- elaborated in detail -- Cooperation Committee --targeted on genuine need to counter disease -- real benefits over time >>health, prosperity	International Cooperation -- not elaborated in detail -- no provision for Cooperation Committee

Organisation -- CoSP, ExC & Technical Secretariat -- TS has role to analyse epidemiological info	Organisation -- CoSP, ExC & Technical Secretariat -- no parallel role
Confidentiality Provisions -- elaborated in detail in Article and Annex	Confidentiality Provisions -- no Article but an Annex -- not as elaborate
National implementation -- Penal legislation required -- National Authority	National implementation -- Penal legislation required -- National Authority

* Indicates that only select facilities meeting certain combinations of conditions, not all such facilities are to be declared.

The CWC verification process has features that can be highlighted to emphasise the point that there are some lessons that the BTWC Protocol can derive from the CWC to be potentially suitable for military use. A small number of chemicals have essential toxicity and the physical properties but developing novel agents is possible. The range of potential biological agents is almost unlimited because of the emergence of natural diseases and the potential for genetic manipulation of micro organisms and toxins. The implications for the BWC protocol on verification is that the purpose based coverage of prohibitions in Article 1 of the BTWC, viz. 'the general purpose criterion' has to be preserved.

A militarily significant quantity of agents would require 80 to 1000 metric tonnes of chemical agents, depending on its type and lethality, while tens of kilograms of toxins and agents are sufficient for mass destructions. The implications for the BTWC Verification Protocol are that significant production of biological and toxin agents in small-scale facilities may elude detection. Military stockpiles have to, of course, remain small enough to permit easy concealment.[10]

---

9. Jonathan B. Tucker, "Verification Provisions of the Chemical Weapons Convention and Their Relevance to the Biological Weapons Convention", in Graham S. Pearson, Gillian R. Woolett, Marie I. Chevrier, Jonathan B. Tucker and Amy E. Smithson, *Biological Weapons Proliferations: Reasons for Concern, Courses of Action*, (Washington DC: Stimson Centre Report) available at http://www.stimson.org/cbw/pdf/report24-entire.pdf, accessed on 20 August 2002.

10. *Ibid*

On the issue of the size of the production facility, a full-scale agent production facility for chemical weapons would require a fairly large industrial site. While in the use of biological weapons, a biological agent production facility could be confined to a small warehouse building if continuous-flow fermentors were used. The implication for the BTWC verification protocol is that clandestine production of biological agents remains hard to detect without human intelligence (retired or defected scientists who could carry biased opinions or could have a vested interest in revelations) which could be unreliable.[11]

On the issue of peaceful medical application of agents and materials, very small quantities of chemical weapons, are used in biomedical research and medical therapeutics. On the other hand, microbial pathogens maybe grown in large quantities for the production of vaccines. Additionally, natural toxins such as botuilinum and ricin are increasingly being used in medical therapeutics. The implication for the BTWC Verification Protocol is that production of microbial pathogens and toxins for legitimate medical purposes can serve as a cover for acquiring a biological weapons capability.[12]

For chemical weapons specialised containment measures and verification systems at production facilities are required only at the final stage of production. These demands can be reduced through production of binary warfare agents. In the case of biological agents containment is primarily needed for steps that generate agent aerosols, such as drying and milling.[13]

On the issue of proprietary sensitivity most chemical products are not highly proprietary. The main concern of the industry is protection of unpatented or non-patentable manufacturing processes. In the case of biological micro-organisms, new drugs, and the pharmaceutical industry's manufacturing processes are highly proprietary and huge sums of money are at stake in their protection. The implication of this for the BTWC protocol on verification is that measures and procedures are required to safeguard confidential proprietary information.[14]

---

11. *Ibid.*
12. *Ibid.*
13. *Ibid.*
14. *Ibid.*

On the issue of physical forms of agents suitable for delivery, chemical agents can be delivered as a liquid mist, vapour or aerosol or as a fine powder (dusty agents). Droplet size varies depending on the volatility of the agent and its ability to penetrate the skin. On the other hand, biological weapons and toxin agents generally cannot penetrate unbroken skin, but could be inhaled, ingested, or injected. Only microscopic particles are retained in the lungs. Large area dispersal would call for a particulate aerosol of dried agent (in powder form) or wet agent (slurry). Of course, dry agents are easier to aerosolise. The implication of this for the BTWC Verification Protocol is that delivery of biological toxins as a respirable aerosol is the only effective means of inflicting mass causalities. This means that equipment for drying microbial cultures (e.g. freeze driers) or the presence of aerosol chambers for testing agent dissemination, maybe tell tale signs of weaponisation.[15]

On the issue of input-output ratio of precursor materials to products, the volume of chemical precursors is directly proportional to the amount of agent produced. In biological weapons, on the other hand, only a small quantity of seed culture can be cultivated in a fermentor and its inherent biological properties will ensure that the culture multiplies. The implication of this for the BTWC protocol on verification is that imposing threshold limits on quantities of biological precursor materials or products is not a feasible monitoring approach.

On the issue of dual-use production equipment and ease of converting a commercial facility to illicit production, nerve agents require corrosion-resistant vessels and special containment and ventilation systems, although some countries may cut corners on worker safety and environmental protection. Conversion of a pesticide plant to a nerve-agent plant would take several weeks. On the other hand, fermentation equipment used to make vaccines, antibiotics and other legitimate products can easily be converted to production of warfare agents. Biocontainment measures are advisable, but not essential, assuming vaccination of plant workers. Conversion of a vaccine plant to biological agent production would take about a week, and periodic manufacture could occur in an ostensibly civilian facility. The implication of this for the BTWC protocol on verification is that the intent to produce biological

15. *Ibid.*

weapons cannot be easily inferred from dual-capable production capabilities. Moreover, supply-side approaches such as non-proliferation export controls are unlikely to be effective over the long term.[16]

On the issue of the size of a relevant commercial industry, dual-capable chemical weapons production facilities are ubiquitous in a large, worldwide chemical industry while in the case of biological weapons dual capable facilities are also ubiquitous in the rapidly expanding, worldwide pharmaceutical and biotechnology industries. The implication of this for the BTWC protocol on verification is that monitoring all potentially relevant dual-capable production sites would be difficult given the limited financial and human resources available.[17]

On the issue of the availability of analytical methods to detect illicit agents, known chemical warfare agents can be reliably detected and identified with analytical techniques such as combined gas chromatography and mass spectrometry. In the case of biological weapons each microbial or toxin agent requires specific antibodies or DNA probes for detection. However, biotechnology may offer ways to develop genetically modified agents that are undetectable by routine testing. Some agents (e.g. anthrax) may also be present naturally in the environment in low concentrations, complicating the interpretations of results. The implication of this for the BTWC Protocol on verification is that sampling and analysis for biological warfare agents requires advance knowledge of which agents are likely to be present. Control samples may also be required to rule out natural sources of contamination. Still, the potential for false-positive or false-negative results means that evidence obtained by sampling and analysis must be corroborated with information from other sources, such as interviews, visual inspection, and audits of production records.[18]

On the ability to clean up a production facility to prevent detection of chemical weapons, a thorough clean-up of a nerve-agent production facility to remove all traces of contamination is difficult because of their durability and persistence of the carbon-phosphorous bond characteristic of nerve agents. On the other hand, in biological weapons, a dual-use

16. *Ibid.*
17. *Ibid.*
18. *Ibid.*

facility such as a vaccine plant could be cleaned manually up in about 8-10 hours. Even so, thorough cleaning may require the disassembly of fermentor systems. Also, residual DNA molecules may be detectable with advanced analytical techniques even after routine sterilisation. The implication of this for the BTWC protocol is that the shorter the advance warning prior to a challenge inspection of a suspected biological-weapons production facility, the greater the probability that clean up will be incomplete and that inspectors will detect traces of illicit agents.[19]

The BTWC Protocol regime has to be unique to the BTWC, and can bring about significant benefits. It requires mandatory declarations of facilities that are of relevance to the Convention: biodefence facilities, BL-4 maximum containment facilities, certain BL-3 high containment facilities with specified production capabilities or engaged in genetic modification, plant pathogen containment facilities, work with listed agents and/or toxins involving production above a certain capacity, genetic modification activities or aerosolisation, and production facilities in excess of certain capacities or producing human or animal vaccines. These declarations must be underpinned by measures to ensure submission with penalties, both automatic and after consideration for late submission. Then there are structured follow-up activities after submission of declarations including randomly-selected transparency visits skewed to avoid any undue burden on any State Party. The effectiveness and efficiency of such transparency visits have been demonstrated in trial visits carried out by several States, frequently with observers present from other States. There are also structured provisions for clarification of any ambiguity, uncertainty, anomaly or omission in a declaration. Then the provisions for addressing concerns about non-compliance include consultation procedures and provisions for field investigations (including release of agents) and facility investigations. These compliance measures are complemented by technical cooperation and assistance provisions that focus on a real need the countering of infectious diseases that will, over time, help States Parties develop the national infrastructure for health. In addition, because of increased transparency and the involvement of national health, safety and quality authorities, this also contributes over time to increased security.

---

19. *Ibid.*

From this discussion it is clear that the BTWC Protocol regime can function in parallel with the CWC regime for monitoring compliance in respect of dual-purpose agents. Whilst the Protocol could have been stronger, it is believed, pragmatically speaking, that further measures to strengthen the Protocol is not likely to be popular and thus that the composite Protocol text is the best that can be negotiated at this time. More negotiation would not strengthen the Composite Protocol text and can at best strengthen some of the existing provisions but could well lead to unravelling what is already a good Protocol. The Protocol regime will significantly augment the non-proliferation regime addressing the total prohibition of biological weapons. The future organisation to implement the Protocol will also bring significant benefits to the regime as it will collect information from States Parties and assist them in achieving effective national implementation measures.

Conclusion

Some states, especially the US felt that it could not support the Draft Protocol, as it would not improve its ability to verify BWC compliance.[20] The US thinks that intrusive on-site inspections 'may not provide useful, accurate and complete information'.[21] The US also believes there is no 'hope that any attempt at a comprehensive declaration inventory would be accurate, timely, or enduringly comprehensive'.[22] It was of the opinion that even after a comprehensive listing of all 'sites', it was possible for a nation to cheat given the dual-use nature of biological agents. This, the US thinks, would not deter non-state actors.[23] The US also assumes that the safeguards that have been inserted would remain insufficient to eliminate unacceptable risks to proprietary or national security information.[24]

There is a tendency for countries to favour verification proposals that do not have much impact on themselves. This would indicate that there are states that believe they are unlikely to face the BW threat to their territories.

---

20. See 'Statement by the United States to the Ad Hoc Group of Biological Weapons Convention States Parties', *Official Text,* Public Affairs Office, US, 25 July 2001, Geneva.
21. *Ibid.*
22. *Ibid.*
23. *Ibid.*
24. *Ibid.*

But verification regimes have to enhance both international and national security by giving states the confidence that violations can be detected and action taken to minimise their effect and to deter potential violators. An important point here is that verification also involves costs, economic and in terms of possible risks to a country's security and legitimate industrial activity. The Draft Protocol in its present form is the best that can be negotiated, and States need to strengthen the present regime than look for alternate solutions.

BWC State Implementation: National Legislation to Deal with the Situation- Can They Substitute the Protocol?

G. Balachandran

Control of WMDs (weapons of mass destruction) and their technologies, denial of technologies to developing countries, especially those that have the potential and desire to develop their national competence in high technologies, has been one the hallmarks of the efforts of the US and its close allies in constructing international conventions and treaties for controlling WMD proliferation.

To attain their goals, these countries have adopted a two-pronged strategy. The first is to fashion international legal instruments to ban or prohibit the possession of WMDs and, secondly, to form cartels with like-minded countries to deny access to dual-use technologies to countries outside the cartel. The technology denial cartels are the Nuclear Suppliers Group (NSG) in the case of dual-use nuclear technologies and the Australia Group (AG) dealing with chemical and biological technologies. In fashioning these international arrangements the primary objectives of the US and its allies have been to devise a system of verification to assure themselves that no prohibited activity takes, or can take place in any country of concern. This requires that a strict protocol exists for verification of any complaints regarding non-compliance with the terms of the treaty.

In the case of nuclear technology, 187 of the 190 member states of the UN are party to the NPT that entered into force in March 1970. Except for the five NPT defined nuclear weapon states, US, Russia, China, France and UK, all others have foregone their nuclear option of nuclear weapons and have signed fullscope safeguards agreements with the IAEA, placing all their nuclear activities under its inspection regime. While the original safeguards agreement was in respect of only special nuclear materials[1],

1. The structure and content of Agreements Between the Agency and States Required in Connection with the Treaty on the Non-Proliferation of Nuclear Weapons, IAEA, INFCIRC/153 (Corrected) June 1972.

after the Gulf War, the IAEA, under pressure from the US and its friends, expanded the scope of safeguards in line with NSG requirements in 1992. Hence NPT members were asked to adopt Additional Protocols[2]. However, because of the sweeping nature of the proposed safeguards only 26 contracting parties have ratified it, even though a large number — 64 in all—had signed it. Dr. Hans Blix, the then Director General of IAEA testified before a US Senate Committee that, "It (IAEA) is your (US) instrument and you can use this for national security."[3] In the matter of additional information sought by the IAEA, Dr. Blix stated, "The information that I am suggesting to member states that they should give to us for safeguards purposes is not going to the Board of Governors but to the Secretariat (of IAEA)"[4], which of course, is heavily staffed by the US and its close allies.

In the case of the Chemical Weapons Convention (CWC), the Protocol agreed upon had a mechanism for verification of prohibited activities in member States in contravention of the requirements of the CWC. The CWC entered into force in April 1997.The mechanism agreed to by the States Parties had a degree of transparency and equity, with an independent mentoring agency able effectively discharge its duties. Here again, according to reports, the US was unhappy with the functioning of the Director General of the Organisation for the Prevention of Chemical Warfare (OPCW) and, with the support of its close friends, ousted him. This was the first time that a Director General of a UN agency was fired midterm. Apparently, the US was angered by Bustani's (the OPCW DG) attempts to persuade Iraq to join the OPCW, and "hardliners in Washington feared Iraq's membership in the OPCW, which would subject it to the organisation's own chemical weapons inspections, might undercut their plans to topple Saddam Hussein on the grounds that he was keeping international weapons inspectors out."[5] The CWC currently has 146 member states.

---

2. Model Protocol Additional to the Agreement(s) between State(s) and the International Atomic Energy Agency for the application of Safeguards., IAEA, INFCIRC/540.
3. Dr. Hans Blix's testimony, itself unprecedented for the head of an UN agency to present himself before a national body. *Committee on Foreign Relations,* US Senate, "Nuclear Proliferation: Learning from Iraq Experience", 17-23 October 1991, pp. 37
4. *Ibid* pp. 40.
5. "US diplomatic might irks nations" Peter Ford, *Christian Science Monitor,* 24 April , 2002.

The Biological Weapons Convention came into force in March 1975. Unlike the NPT and the CWC which, from the very beginning, had a verification mechanism built into the treaty, the BWC lacked even basic verification and enforcement mechanisms. As a result, even though there were serious accusations that the Soviet Union was engaged in massive BW research, nothing could be done. While the West ascribed the 1979 anthrax outbreak in the Soviet city of Sverdlovsk (now Yekaterinberg) to a release from an illegal Soviet BW facility, the Soviets argued that it was due to contaminated meat. The issue could not be resolved because of the absence of any verification procedure in the BWC[6].

Thus, while there was some concern about the lack of any verification mechanism, it was not until the 1991 Gulf War, when it became known that Iraq was actively pursuing a BW programme, that members of the BWC began to be seriously concerned. This resulted in the establishment of a Verification Experts group called VEREX. A special conference was convened in Geneva in September 1994 to consider its report.[7] It established an Ad Hoc Group (AHG), to draft proposals to strengthen the BWC, and develop a legally binding document. At the Fourth Review Conference (1996) the States Parties agreed that a Special Conference be held to consider the Ad Hoc Group's report, including the Verification Protocol, to be held as soon as possible before the Fifth Review Conference.

The AHG held a large number of sessions in the subsequent period the last one being the 24th session from 23 July to 17 August 2001. It could not agree on a protocol - the so - called "rolling text" - acceptable to all. Accordingly, Ambassador Tibor Toth, Chairman of the AHG drafted a composite Protocol Text in March 2001 which was based on the "rolling text" of the protocol. At the 24th session more than 50 of the 55 states engaged in the negotiations stated that the Chairman's composite protocol should form the basis for political decisions to adopt the protocol before the Fifth Review Conference. The US delegate, however affirmed that, "After extensive deliberation, the United States has concluded that the

6. In October 1996, Cuba alleged that the US had wilfully released a biological agent against crops known as thrips palmi in the province of Matanzas. This too could not be investigated.
7. Final declaration of the Special Conference (VEREX), BWC/SPCONF/ 1 September 1994.

current approach to a Protocol to the Biological Weapons Convention, an approach most directly embodied in CRP.8, known as the "Composite Text," is not, in our view, capable of achieving the mandate set forth for the Ad Hoc Group, strengthening confidence in compliance with the Biological Weapons Convention. .... we will therefore be unable to support the current text, even with changes, as an appropriate outcome of the Ad Hoc Group efforts."

Nevertheless, President Bush in a statement on 1 November 2001, following the anthrax attacks in the United States, stated, "Our objective is to fashion an effective international approach to strengthen the Biological Weapons Convention."[8]

At the Fifth Review Conference in November 2001 the US categorically rejected the composite text stating , "We will continue to reject flawed texts like the BWC Draft Protocol, recommended to us simply because they are the product of lengthy negotiations or arbitrary deadlines, if such texts are not in the best interests of the United States and many other countries represented here today." In addition, the US levelled serious charges against Iraq, Iran, North Korea, Libya, Sudan, and Syria, stating that they were engaged in BW programmes. The US did make some suggestions on how to strengthen the BWC in the areas of i) national implementation, ii) consultation and cooperation and iii) assistance to victims, and iv) technical and scientific cooperation. It was clear that no consensus could be reached at the Review Conference, and it was accordingly adjourned to reconvene at Geneva from 11 to 22 November 2002.

This paper will discuss the question of National Implementation requirements of the BWC (Article IV) which is a prime requirement of the US. Article IV of the Biological and Toxin Weapons Convention requires that, "Each State Party shall, in accordance with its constitutional processes, take any necessary measures to prohibit and prevent the development, production, stockpiling, acquisition or retention of the agents, toxins, weapons, equipment and means of delivery specified in Article I of the Convention, within the territory of such State, under its

---

8. The White House, Statement by the President: Strengthening the International regime against Biological Weapons", 1 November 2001.

jurisdiction or under its control anywhere." Unfortunately not many State Parties have complied with this requirement. Would compliance with Article. IV itself be sufficient to substitute for the protocol? The simple answer is: No.

Any successful BWC Protocol must reflect two critical interests of the State Parties to the BWC:

1) The need to bolster confidence in compliance, the prime concern of the US; and
2) The need to strengthen provisions regarding biological-related cooperation for peaceful purposes

The second requirement is the one that is most keenly felt by the developing countries, who need to be assured that the new regime will not be used to deny them critical technologies in the future. Their past experience in matters of technology transfer and scientific cooperation have not been encouraging. The NPT, for example, assured the State Parties that "All the parties to the Treaty undertake to facilitate, and have the right to participate in, the fullest possible exchange of equipment, materials and scientific and technical information for the peaceful uses of nuclear energy. Parties to the Treaty in a position to do so shall also cooperate in contributing...to the further development of applications of nuclear energy for peaceful purposes, especially in the territories of non-nuclear-weapon States Party to the Treaty, with due consideration for the needs of the developing areas of the world."[9] In practice the results have been disheartening. Nuclear power constitutes a major peaceful use of nuclear energy. Many countries in Europe depend on nuclear power for their electricity requirements.

Yet, instead of adhering honestly with the requirements of Article IV, the west and its allies have taken refuge under Article. I, of the NPT which states "each nuclear-weapon State Party to the Treaty undertakes not to transfer to any recipient whatsoever nuclear weapon or other nuclear explosive devices or control over such weapons or explosive devices directly, or indirectly." Nuclear technology denial regimes like the NSG have been controlling and denying dual-use items on the grounds that they might contribute indirectly to such programmes, since they are dual-use items!

---

9. Article IV (2) of the Treaty on the Non-proliferation of Nuclear Weapons.

A similar situation obtains regarding the BWC as well. While Article. X of the BWC is almost identical to Article. 4 of the NPT[10], there is an article similar to Article 1 of the NPT.[11] However, unlike nuclear technology, biotechnology has applications in areas of health, and agriculture. There also exists a restrictive technology cartel, the Australia group, which has adopted a very stringent denial-prone technology transfer regime. Since 11 September, the group has focused on revamping its control lists to better address the terrorist threat. In 2002, the AG adopted licensing guidelines and became the first regime to require participants to have catch-all controls (covering *non-AG listed* items when destined for CBW use and to control *intangible transfers* of technology). The AG also agreed to control technology for the development and production of listed biological agents and equipment. In recent years, AG members have begun to consider measures to address the challenges posed by cooperation on CBW programmes by non-member countries. In short, under the rules followed by AG members even training of students in these technologies could be restricted as representing "intangible transfers". The AG has been criticised by members of the developing world in both BWC and CWC forums, but with little effect. There is a real danger that the AG may become even more restrictive in future, precisely because of the rapid developments in biotechnology.

Considering the fact that the Biological sciences, especially biotechnology, are in the forefront of the technologies of the future. There is a real danger the developing countries will be left at the mercy of

10. Article X. of BWC which states "(1) The States Parties to this Convention undertake to facilitate, and have the right to participate in, the fullest possible exchange of equipment, materials and scientific and technological information for the use of bacteriological (biological) agents and toxins for peaceful purposes. Parties to the Convention in a position to do so shall also cooperate in contributing individually or together with other States or international organisations to the further development and application of scientific discoveries in the field of bacteriology (biology) for prevention of disease, or for other peaceful purposes."

11. Article III of the BWC states, "Each State Party to this Convention undertakes not to transfer to any recipient whatsoever, directly or indirectly, and not in any way to assist, encourage, or induce any State, group of States or international organisations to manufacture or otherwise acquire any of the agents, toxins, weapons, equipment or means of delivery specified in Article I of this Convention."

the West. Unless there is a legally binding protocol which has greater assurance of technology support and cooperation than has been forthcoming, there is very little incentive for the developing cantries to agree to stringent National Implementation regulations to provide confidence to the West about compliance. There is an even more disturbing fact. It is very unlikely that any internationally agreed compliance procedure and actions will satisfy the US. The Iraq experience provides a classic example that without a protocol a country can easily undertake a BW programme without any danger of being exposed; and at the same time a powerful country can ignore all inspections and insist on an unlimited duration of verification tests and continued presence of international inspectors without an end in sight. Now there are persistent demands for return of the IAEA inspectors to Iraq to continue with their OMV (Onsite Monitoring and Verification) in Iraq. Indeed the bogey of a nuclear Iraq is frequently raised as a justification for military action, against all international norms against it.[12]

Unlike verification of nuclear material which is fairly easy, there being installations like reactors, enrichment facilities and reprocessing plants that are visible, the facilities that can have potential BW related activities are many, and their size of operations need not be large. Further, the range of industrial activities that can be potentially useful for BW work is very large. A whole range of peaceful activities, even a simple facility producing yogurt, for example, can potentially engage in BW activities. Therefore, it is well nigh impossible to prove to everybody's satisfaction that no BW work is being done in a country. Certainly, no National Implementation rules, regulations, procedures etc. will convince a country like the US if it chooses to target a specific country as being inimical to its national interests. Nor should one assume that the compliance "certificate" so to speak, after appropriate verification procedures are in place, will be considered acceptable.

The case of Iran is another example. Iran is a member of good standing with IAEA and has a fullscope safeguards agreement with IAEA. IAEA has routinely conducted safeguards verification inspections in Iran and has certified that Iran is in full compliance with its agreement. Yet the US

---

12. The latest being the dossier brought out by the British Government, "Iraq's weapons of mass destruction: The assessment of the British government".

regularly alleges that Iran is conducting a NW programme.[13] Nor should one take consolation that the US is only concerned with countries it had designated as "rogue states". The new term is "countries of concern". Under such circumstances National Implementation procedures will neither be necessary nor sufficient to assist a country in establishing its compliance with the BWC if the US or its major allies choose to level charges against it. Nor will such National Implementation procedures protect it, if the US chooses to exercise its military option in a unilateral, or illegal manner. The recently released National Security Strategy of the United States makes it abundantly clear that the US can exercise its military options against any country which it feels may threaten its security. As the document makes clear, "The United States can no longer solely rely on a reactive posture as we have in the past. The inability to deter a potential attacker, the immediacy of today's threats, and the magnitude of potential harm that could be caused by our adversaries' choice of weapons, do not permit that option. We cannot let our enemies strike first….. The greater the threat, the greater is the risk of inaction—and the more compelling the case for taking anticipatory action to defend ourselves… To forestall or prevent such hostile acts by our adversaries, the United States will, if necessary, act preemptively."[14]

Given the nature of biotechnology and related sciences and their potential advance in the coming years there is little doubt that BWs will be considered an alternative to defence against predatory countries. Also given the nature of the science, it will be very difficult to establish conclusively that one is not engaged in BW activities. It is also apparent that the US, along with its allies, will attempt to deny any technology that may be considered as dual-use BW technology, to countries that are allied to it. Whether it will succeed in its attempts to hold back the technological development of the countries it fears, is doubtful. Ironically, the more it fails, the more paranoid it will become. Given such an environment, while a BWC Protocol may not be entirely foolproof, it will at least assure the international community that the norms against BW

---

13. It is ironical that Iran which is a member of all the three WMD related international conventions, the NPT, the CWC and the BWC, is pilloried as a rogue state while, Israel, which is not even a signatory to any of these treaties and is known to possess nuclear weapons, is hailed as a "major US ally."
14. The National Security Strategy of the United States, p. 15.

are in place. Any such protocol must address both the issues of compliance and technology cooperation to ensure stability as regards non-proliferation of BWs.

A protocol without US participation will not last long. Nor will it last long, if the US does not agree to abide by accepted international norms on interstate relations, equity in the sharing of knowledge and refrain from unilateral military action against alleged infractions. Without a protocol, no amount of National Implementation procedures, rules and regulations will assure a country of its share of the fruits of knowledge. An effective National Implementation system in accordance with Article IV is necessary for a successful Protocol, but a Protocol without provisions for a satisfactory transfer of technology to developing countries in accordance with Article X will not ensure a lasting one.

This is not to deny that it is in each country's own national interests to have domestic laws to prevent the development or production of BW agents within its territory or under its control. But in what form and shape these laws are enacted is dependent on the national security requirements of that country and not in response to any uniform global system, except in the context of a BWTC protocol.

Compulsions of the Biotech Industry/ Reservations Regarding the BTWC Protocol and Suggested Solutions

Sandhya Tewari
Divya Chopra

Advances in the biotechnology sector, including the progress in the sphere of recombinant DNA technology, has brought numerous benefits and much growth; however, it has also created the ability to misuse this development by enhancing the threat of biological and chemical warfare. It is important, therefore, for scientists in this area to understand the implications of their work.

Likewise, arms control experts must recognise that there is a profound revolution underway in biology and that the technical landscape of chemical and biological arms control is rapidly changing. These rapid advances by the biotechnology sector in the last five decades have highlighted the need to review international conventions and protocols.

The Biological and Toxins Weapons Convention (BTWC) was opened for signature in 1972 and entered into force in 1975. India, along with 143 other countries, is party to this Convention.

The basic obligation of the Convention is the undertaking not to "develop, produce, stockpile or otherwise retain (a) microbial or other biological agents, or toxins, whatever their origins or method of production, of types and in quantities that have no justification for prophylactic, protective or other peaceful purposes..." With developments in recombinant DNA technology, the need was felt for strengthening the Convention. For the last five years, negotiations have been underway in Geneva, "to strengthen the effectiveness and improve the implementation of the Convention by considering appropriate measures, including measures relating to verification, in the form of a legally binding instrument, referred to as the BW Protocol."

Key Elements of the Protocol

The key elements of the protocol are the following:

- States Parties to make declarations, on an annual basis, relating to biological containment facilities, which are pharmaceuticals facilities above a certain size and organisations working with any of the biological agents or toxins that are listed in the protocol.

- Declarations to be submitted to an international secretariat. Verification of declarations will take place through a combination of the process of consultation and clarification as well as visits to facilities.

- Provisions for protection of commercially sensitive information are also part of the protocol. These visits can range from transparency-related visits for building confidence to *investigative visits* where there is an apprehension of a serious violation of the basic objectives of the convention. The equipment to be carried by the inspection team, decision-making on the report, etc. are all aspects of the ongoing negotiations.

Cooperative and effective verification mechanisms are a must for the protocol to be effective.

Declarations for a range of activities and facilities are listed in the protocol:

- Past offensive BW programme
- Past defensive BW programme
- Present defensive BW programme
- BSL-4 / BSL-3 facilities
- Vaccine production facility
- Plant pathogen containment facility
- Work with listed agents and toxins
- Other production facilities involving micro-organisms
- Other facilities that includes aerosolisation and genetic engineering work in BSL-3 facility
- Transfers
- Outbreak of disease

The first and second items require one time declaration, others need annual declarations. Declarations will be made in a format that is being standardised in Geneva.

Visits

The Protocol envisages three kinds of visits:

- Randomly selected visits
- Voluntary clarification visits
- Voluntary assistance visits

Investigations

These are of two types in the Protocol:

- Field investigation: aim to find out whether the use of BW has indeed occurred and is so, by whom and when.
- Facility investigation: aim to find out whether there is any non-compliance concern such as production or stockpiling of biological weapons or agents.

Confidentiality

Taking into consideration the concerns expressed by the industry, viz. loss of proprietary information during declarations and on site visits, an article and annex on confidentiality were added to the protocol. To ensure that breaches of confidentiality are dealt with in an unbiased manner, a body called Confidentiality Commission would be established, which will go into such breaches between State Parties and between a State Party and the organisation.

Indian Industry's Apprehension: Striking a Balance

Outcome of the negotiations on the protocol will have a bearing on India's small but rapidly growing bio-tech industry. In view of growing appreciation worldwide of the danger of the misuse of biological materials, the industry is fully aware that more regulations and controls will be required in future. This is quite acceptable to those working in what is already a very highly regulated industry.

The central elements of the protocol that are of great concern to the biotech and pharmaceutical industry relate to the requirements of declarations, the procedure of visits to facilities, and the provisions for safeguarding of confidentiality. The basic concern of the industry is that the declaration provisions will not impose a significant additional burden upon industry. Striking a balance, therefore, becomes extremely important.

Awareness of the Provisions of the Protocols and Implications for the Industry

There is, however, very little awareness about the ongoing negotiations and the provisions of the Protocol in the Indian Industry. A Seminar on "Implications of BTWC for Indian Biotech and Pharma Industry" conducted by the Confederation of Indian Industry in April 2001 served to create awareness about the Protocol and helped to inform the relevant biotech and pharmaceutical organisations about its implications for them. The main objective was to discuss the strengthened BTWC Protocol and create synergy between the biotech and pharma industries as well as the concerned government departments and ministries to work towards an active Indian position on the negotiations.

Subsequent to this initiative, the Confederation of Indian Industry established a dedicated Task Force on BTWC, comprising representatives from Industry, MEA, DRDO and DBT. This task force keeps the industry informed about the negotiations going on in Geneva, assesses their implications as they evolve and exchanges views with similar organisations in other countries.

CII Survey to Assess Implications for the Industry

There has been much debate and different positions being taken with respect to the BTWC Protocol. CII has attempted to work on the most stringent version of this draft before June 2001.

A survey was conducted by the CII by circulation of a questionnaire that was designed to assess the present status of security and adherence to policy in the various industries involved. In essence, it was intended to check how many industries/ institutions would come under the purview of the protocol in terms of declarations. The main issues focused upon in the questionnaire were as follows:

- Production of vaccines against human or animal disease;
- Check for maximum biological containment (BSL-3) / high biological containment (BSL-4) / plant pathogen containment facility;

- Check-list of agents and toxins, viz. human and zoonotic pathogens, animal pathogens, plant pathogens, and toxins;
- Check - list to determine whether work with any of the toxins falls within acceptable categories, for example, BSL-3 facility;
- Check for the usage of aerosol test chamber of 100 l. of aerosol dissemination apparatus;
- Conducting of genetic modification with any organism in a BSL-3 facility;
- Modification of DNA/RNA sequence of agents for coding of toxins;
- Insertion of nucleic acid sequence of agents for coding into any other organism;
- Maintenance of culture collection of these agents in BSL-4 or BSL-3 facility;
- Check for production of chemicals or other pharma products / biocontrol agents or plant inoculants / diagnostic reagents using micro-organisms.

The questionnaire was analysed to assess the position of the Indian industry with regard to coming under the purview of declarations. Twenty-seven industries / research laboratories/ independent institutes/ university departments participated in the survey (broadly divided into Industry and Research Body/Institute). The results of the survey revealed that over 85 per cent of the participants in the survey would come under their purview, and only 4 (15 per cent) would be outside the purview of the declarations.

The Future

While the BTWC negotiations were on for the last 6½ years, the US Administration questioned the Protocol in June 2001. However, the 11 September and the anthrax attacks that followed necessitated a review of the issues included in the Verification Protocol.

The US President's office issued a press release stressing the urgent need for a concerted effort to fight bioterrorism in November 2001. These statements were made with the objective "to fashion an effective international approach to strengthen the Convention against the threat of biological weapons."

In summary, the following proposals were made by the US administration:

- Enact strict national criminal legislation against prohibited activities with strong extradition requirements;
- Establish an effective United Nations procedure for investigating suspicious outbreaks or allegations of biological weapons use;
- Establish procedures for addressing BWC compliance concerns;
- Commit to improving international disease control and enhance mechanisms for sending expert response teams to cope with outbreaks;
- Establish sound national oversight mechanisms for the security and genetic engineering of pathogenic organisms;
- Devise a solid framework for bioscientists in the form of a code of ethical conduct that would have universal recognition; and
- Promote responsible conduct in the study, use, modification, and shipment of pathogenic organisms.

These points are likely to form the basis of future negotiations.

The viewpoint and concerns of the Indian Biotech and Pharmaceutical Industry may be best understood through the following deliberations;

Industry strongly realises and recognises that the Protocol must be stringent to be effective.

It was agreed that the prohibited activities aforementioned should be made criminal offences instead of civil liabilities, and any potential biological warfare (BW) oriented activity or use of agents should only be carried out only under strict surveillance. For this purpose, a clear declaration of prohibited BW activities should be put in place.

The Indian industry is also of the view that an effective UN Procedure must be established to investigate suspicious outbreaks or allegations of BW use, though natural outbreaks of disease should be excluded.

With respect to procedures put into place for addressing BWC compliance concerns, the earlier deliberations in the BTWC stated that such visits had to be approved by the entire committee of 52 participating countries. However, the proposal now is that if a country A is suspicious of another country B's activities, it may ask B for an explanation, failing which an inspection team may be sent there, and B would have to oblige.

Indian industry is of the opinion that this provision should be formulated in such a way that it is not used arbitrarily.

Other concerns of the industry relate to the confidentiality of the company being investigated. The following points should be taken care of:

1. The protocol should declare that inspections would be carried out only after adequate declarations are sought and only against suspicion.

2. The inspection thus carried out should only be visual in nature with no photographs or any other records being taken.

3. The facilities that come under the purview of inspections should be clearly defined. The base should be:

    a) Fermenters with capacities above fifty litres;

    b) Only P4 laboratories should come under purview;

    c) Facilities using organisms which could be used for biological warfare should fall under the purview of inspections.

Indian industry is of the view that the guidelines for inspection should be so formulated that they do not conflict with the confidentiality concerns of any company.

Further, to the objective of enhancing facilities of international disease control, Indian industry is of the opinion that there should be a commitment to improving international disease control and to enhance mechanisms for sending expert response teams to cope with outbreaks.

Presently all companies in India that use recombinant DNA technologies report to either the Institutional Biosafety Committee (IBSC), Review Committee for Genetically Modified Products (RCGM) or Genetic Engineering. The Approval Committee (GEAC) exists for purposes of ensuring biosafety before their products are released in the market. Still the system for ensuring biosafety is inadequate, which was recently highlighted when an Indian company could not export a GM drug as prior approval was required from the WHO stating that the exporting country's regulatory mechanism is satisfactory, and this could not be obtained for India.

Another example was the difficulty in taking penal action against the violators of these regulations – as can be seen from the Gujarat cotton case, where genetically modified seeds were sold to farmers and planted without getting approval from the concerned authorities. The solution lies in India having a strong regulatory mechanism in place, and in streamlining the definition of pathogens at the international level.

India's export controls relevant to the BTWC state that Export of Special Chemicals, Organisms, Materials, Equipment and Technologies (SCOMET) would be permitted under certain categories only against an export license issued in this behalf unless it is prohibited or permitted without a license, subject to the fulfilment of conditions if any, indicated for any specific category. The Indian industry is of the opinion that while *adequate measures* should be taken to prevent abuse of biological products through the Convention, care should also be taken to address developing countries' industry concerns.

It is important to note that industry is aware of the problems, as also the benefits of such a Protocol. This is a scenario that is and must be driven by confidentiality, but we cannot have weak verification systems. However, the process of destroying evidence of illegal or offensive activity is not a lengthy one, and can easily be affected by a non-complying organisation before visits.

Therefore, it is the actual implementation of the protocol that is the task that lies ahead. There are two obvious reasons for this, namely the fact that the micro-organisms that form the core of BW are found in nature; and technical advances can allow for the production and hiding of illegal materials within a short period of time.

Industry, is thus concerned with the 'method' by which such loopholes can be checked and non-compliance corrected.

To conclude, future negotiations must have in their mandate the devising of measures to protect sensitive commercial proprietary information to avoid any negative impact on industrial development. Further, on the issue of technology transfer, there must be a method for sharing the same. Alternatively, smaller nations should have mechanisms for greater competence building and ability to counter possible aggression.

References

1. A Short Note on Biological Warfare; Dr. R.V. Swamy, Director, Defence Research & Development Establishment, Gwalior (Government of India, Ministry of Defence)

2. The Implications of Biological and Toxin Weapon Convention on Indian Biotechnology and Pharmaceutical Industry; Dr. R.V. Swamy, Director, Defence Research & Development Establishment, Gwalior (Govternment. of India, Ministry of Defence)

3. The Biological and Toxin Weapons Convention
http://projects.sipri.se/cbw/docs/bw-btwc-text.html

4. The Strengthened BTWC Protocol: Implications for the Biotechnology and Pharmaceutical Industry.
http://www.brad.ac.uk/acad/sbtwc/

5. House of Cards: The Pivotal Importance of Technically Sound BWC Monitoring Protocol
http://www.stimson.org/cwc/cards.html

6. White House Press Release, 1 November 2001; Office of International Information Programs, US Department of State

7. Comments, Ambassador Rakesh Sood, Ambassador and Permanent Representative, Permanent Mission of India to the Conference on Disarmament

8. Comments, CII Task Force members

Endgame in November 2002: US Position Other Alternative Modalities to Protocol

Kalpana Chittaranjan

Norms matter in international politics – not because they constrain the choices of the most malevolent of men but because they create the basis for consensus about responses to actions inconsistent with those norms.

Brad Roberts[1]

The last few months have seen the USA and UK making a case for a "regime change" in Iraq, i.e. the removal of President Saddam Hussein on grounds that he possesses weapons of mass destruction (WMD).[2] In an ironic twist to 'today's friends becoming tomorrow's enemies', reports have revealed that the US government once authorised germ cultures capable of being used for biological weapons to Iraq in the 1980s, including pathogens like anthrax, boutlinum toxin and gangrene[3].

Though innate human revulsion against biological weapons has seen to it that biological weapons have rarely been used ,[4] terrorists in the post-

---

1. Brad Roberts, "Implementing the Biological Weapons Convention: Looking Beyond the Verification Issue," in Oliver Thraenert, ed., The Verification of the Biological Weapons Convention: Problems and Perspectives (Bonn: Friedrich Ebert Stiftung, 1992), p. 104.
2. For example, see the White House issued document, A Decade of Deception and Defiance: Saddam Hussein's Defiance of the UN on 12 September 2002, available at : http://www.whitehouse.gov/news/releases/2002/09/iraqdecade.pdf and the UK government issued dossier, Iraq's Weapons of Mass Destruction: The Assessment of the British Government on September 24 2002, available at: http://news.bbc.c..uk/nol/shored/spl/hi/middle_east/02/uk_dossier_on_iraq/pdf/iraqdossier.pdf.
3. Douglas Turner, "US sent Iraq germs in mid-80s,' *The Buffalo News*, 23 September 2002; and Mike Toner, "Backgrounder: Germ Sharing: A Necessary Risk", Atlanta Journal-Constitution, 2 October 2002.
4. For a comprehensive review of the use and alleged use of biological weapons over the years, and the likely devastating impact of use of such weapons see Kalpana Chittaranjan, "Biological Weapons: An Insidious WMD", *Strategic Analysis,* Vol.. XXII No. 9, December 1998, pp.1428-1431.

11 September 2001 age may use any weapon and do anything to achieve their objectives. Thus, it is imperative for states and international mechanisms to prevent biological weapons from falling into the hands of state-sponsored terrorism or non-state actors. As the title suggests, this article describes the Bush Administration's position on issues confronting the Biological Weapons Convention (BWC)* and the alternative modalities to a verification protocol (VP).

Biological and Toxin Weapons Convention[5] The Convention on the Prohibition of the Development, Production, and Stockpiling of Bacteriological (Biological) and Toxin Weapons and on Their Destruction better knows as the Biological and Toxin Weapons Convention or by its acronym BWC, was negotiated from 1969-1971, opened for signature on 10 April 1972 at London, Moscow and Washington DC, and entered into force on 26 March 1975,with 43 member countries, upon ratification by the three depository states — the USA, the former Soviet Union (FSU) and the UK.[6]. As of 31 July 2002, the BWC had 146 state parties that have ratified with 8 other signatories.[7]

From the beginning, the Convention suffered from flaws in not being able to verify or enforce compliance. Its history has therefore been attempts at giving the BWC more teeth to have the means of catching cheaters. Without going into this history, it should be pointed out that an Ad Hoc Group has been trying to develop a Verification Protocol to

---

* Up to *November* 2002.

5. For a more detailed history of the BWC and its workings, see elsewhere in this monograph. Also see Kalpana Chittaranjan, "History of the BTWC and AHG," in P.R.Chari and Arpit Rajain (eds.,) Working Towards a Verification Protocol for Biological Weapons (New Delhi: Institute of Peace and Conflict Studies, July 2001), pp. 9-21; Kalpana Chittaranjan, "The BWC: A Status Report," *Strategic Analysis*, Vol. XXV, No. 2, May 2001, pp. 215-225; Kalpana Chittaranjan, "Verification Protocol: A Must for BWC Effectiveness," *Strategic Analysis*, Vol. XXIII, No. 6, September 1999, pp. 947 – 965.
6. The Arms Control Reporter: A Chronicle of Treaties, Negotiations, Proposals, Weapons and Policy (Massachusetts: IDDS, 1996), p. 701, A1.
7. Ratifications to the BTWC at http://www.projects.sipri.se/cbw/docs/bw-btwc-rat.html as of 31 July 2002. For Fact Sheet on the BWC, see The Biological Weapons Convention at a Glance at http://www.armscontrol.org/factsheets/bwcataglance.asp?print .

implement the BWC. It met for the twenty-third time from 23 April to 11 May 2001 by which time its negotiators had arrived at a 250-page draft, containing over 1000 brackets (indicating points of disagreement), known as the "Rolling Text."[8] However, a 210-page compromise Protocol known as the "Composite Text" was tabled by the Chair of the AHG, Ambassador Tibor Toth of Hungary, on 30 March 2001,[9] three weeks before the start of this session, to try and break the impasse and reduce the points of disagreement. It soon became apparent that this session would be devoted to debating the merits of the rolling text over the composite text as the basis for further negotiation of the draft Verification Protocol. By the end of the session, though, the composite text had become the de facto basis of the Protocol.[10]

The AHG met for its twenty-fourth and last scheduled session from 23 July to 17 August 2001, at Geneva,[11] when US Ambassador Donald Mahley announced on 25 July 2001 that his country could not support the draft Protocol as it would 'not improve our ability to verify compliance' with the BWC's global ban on BW and 'would put national security and confidential business at risk',[12] all hopes for progress at the session vanished. The AHG then began the task of writing its report but failed to reach agreement on it. Thus, it failed in its mandated task of completing negotiations on a Protocol before the Fifth BWC Review was to be held in Geneva between 19 November to 7 December 2001.

As Jenni Rissanen puts it, "The Fifth Review Conference of the Biological and Toxin Weapons Convention closed, as it had opened, in eventful

---

8. Part I and Part II of the Rolling Text Revisions are available in the PDF format from website http://www.fas.org/bwc/protocol.htm.
9. For text, see *ibid.*
10. For an extensive coverage of the twenty-third AHG Session, see Jenni Rissanen, "Hurdles Cleared, Obstacles Remaining: the Ad Hoc Group Prepares for the Final Challenge," *Disarmament Diplomacy,* Issue No. 56, April 2001.
11. For a wide coverage of the twenty-fourth AHG session, see Jenni Rissanen, "A Turning Point to Nowhere? BWC in trouble as US Turns its Back on Verification Protocol," *Disarmament Diplomacy,* Issue No. 59, July-August 2001.
12. Text of *Statement by the United States To the Ad Hoc Group of Biological Weapons Convention State Parties* – Geneva, Switzerland, 25 July 2001, at http://www.usinfo.state.gov/topical/pol/arms/stories/01072501.htm.

and acrimonious fashion."[13] This was because less than two hours before the Review Conference was to end, the US proposed that the Conference terminate the AHG's mandate[14], which would have put a complete stop to a little more than a decade's efforts to strengthen the Convention. In order to prevent outright failure, the ninety-one states that were present, adjourned the Conference until 11-12 November 2002. When the states reconvened in November 2002, they had to decide about the fate of the almost finalised draft Final Declaration,[15] as well as the AHG and its mandate. There were a number of analysts who were quite pessimistic about the outcome in November 2002. Among them, Jez Littlewood[16], as early as July 2002, said, "My personal guess is nothing will come out of the meeting because changes in critical positions have failed to materialise and such changes are necessary if any agreement is to be reached. However, even if very little comes out of Review Conference Part II it will be greeted as a great success. We are in a situation not dissimilar to the Second Review Conference in 1986 when there was widespread concern about the impact of biotechnology and compliance with the treaty but little political will and not many ideas which could generate consensus agreement on how to address the problems.

When the BWC Review Conference met on 11 November 2002 it formally closed on the 15th after agreeing on Chairman Tibor Toth's limited programme of further discussions on addressing the biological weapons threat.[17] Toth's proposal calls for annual meetings of member-states on national measures to implement the BWC as well as measures to control dangerous pathogens and better international response and investigation of alleged use of bioweapons and improved surveillance. Oliver Meier,

---

13. Jenni Rissanen, "Left in Limbo: Review Conference Suspended - On Edge of Collapse," *Disarmament Diplomacy*, Issue No. 62, December-January 2002. See *ibid* for an extensive coverage and BWC Report on the Fifth Review Conference of the BWC.
14. For an immediate reaction to the US action, see Jenni Rissanen, "Anger After the Ambush: Review Conference Suspended After US Asks for AHG's Termination," *BWC Review Conference Bulletin 9* December 2001 at http://www.acronym.org.uk/bwc/revcon8.htm.
15. See "The Draft Final Declaration" *Disarmament, Diplomacy,* Issue No. 62, December-January 2002.
16. Jez Littlewood, Mountbatten Centre for International Studies, UK, via-email dated 30 July 2002.
17. For details, see BWC/CONF.V/17, Final Report para. 18., pp. 3-4.

representative of the Arms Control Association who attended the conference, stated, "The process outlined by Ambassador Toth would limit further international discussions to national and voluntary measures on bioweapons and would not allow for the development of new, legally binding measures to prevent the development and production of biological weapons," he pointed out. "Nevertheless, the agreement is positive because, for the first time, BWC state parties will meet annually to discuss measures to strengthen the ban on bioweapons."[18]

US Stand on Issues Before the BWC

US Position under the Bush Administration : While working towards a draft verification protocol, there was general agreement among member states on the essential need for a verifying and enforcing mechanism to make the BWC effective. However, ever since the Bush Administration took over in January 2001, it was made clear, especially in the 24th AHG session in July-August 2001 and the Fifth Review Conference of the BWC in November-December 2001, that it had completely lost faith in the draft protocol drawn up by the AHG to carry out its stated objectives, and in the mandate of the AHG itself. This stand was surprising given the US anthrax attacks in September-October 2001 as also the likely imminent threat of biological weapons being used against the US. Some analysts feel that these reasons should/would have made the US authorities support the drawing up of a verifying mechanism at the earliest.

Given below are excerpts of key US administration officials[19] statements that make clear the Bush administration's stand on issues before the BWC.

---

18. Arms Control Association, Media Advisory, "Arms Control Experts Call Bio-Weapons Conference Outcome "Useful But Insufficient," 14 November 2002.
19. For more statements by US administration officials, see: "Wolfowitz Cites Importance of Biological Weapons Treaty at http://usinfo.state.gov/topical/pol/arms/stories/01073001.htm; Jenni Rissanen, "United States' Position on Protocol Unmoved," BWC Protocol Bulletin, 15 October 2001 at http://www.acronym.org.uk/bwc/bwc11.htm; News Review – "US Officials Outline Approach to BWC Bioterrorism Challenges," Disarmament Diplomacy, Issue No. 63, March-April 2002; and John R. Bolton, "The New Strategic Framework: A Response to 21st Century Threats," US Foreign Policy Agenda, Vol. 7, No. 2, July 2002, p. 6.

Mahley's Testimony Before the House of Representatives Subcommittee

Ambassador Donald A. Mahley, Special Negotiator for Chemical and Biological Arms Control, gave testimony on 10 July 2001 before The House Government Reform Committee: Subcommittee on National Security, Veteran Affairs and International Relations.[20] He started by clarifying that the US unreservedly supported the BWC.

He went on to add:[21]

...we seek improvement in the ability to impede the threat and reality of biological weapons proliferation in the world. We recognise that there is some risk inherent in any such effort, given the magnitude and advanced state of US biodefence activity and the biotech industry in the United States. What we have sought is a balance that would achieve greater benefit in the non-proliferation and arms control objectives than costs to legitimate national security and commercial interests. That is a judgment that will be made finally at senior political levels of the executive branch...

Mahley's Statement at 24th AHG Session

On 25 July 2001, while announcing that the US would not support the draft protocol, i.e. the "composite text" under consideration before the AHG, Ambassador Mahley said:[22]

One overarching concern is the inherent difficulty of crafting a mechanism suitable to address the unique biological weapons threat. The traditional approach that has worked well for many other types of weapons is not a workable structure for biological weapons. We believe the objective of the mandate was and is important to international security, we will therefore be unable to support the current text, even with changes, as an appropriate outcome of the Ad Hoc Group efforts.

President Bush's Steps to Strengthen Biological Weapons Pact

On 1 November 2001, US President George Bush proposed a series of

20. Full text at: http://.usinfo.state.gov/topical/pol/arms/stories/01071101.htm.
21. *Ibid.*
22. Full text at http://usinfo.state.gov/topical/pol/arms/stories/01072501.htm.

steps that state parties to the BWC could take to strengthen it. While announcing these steps, he said:[23]

The United States is committed to strengthening the Biological Weapons Convention (BWC) as part of a comprehensive strategy for combating the complex threats of weapons of mass destruction and terrorism. With this objective, my Administration is proposing that all Parties:

— Enact strict national criminal legislation against prohibited BW activities with strong extradition requirements;

— Establish an effective United Nations procedure for investigating suspicious outbreaks or allegations of biological weapons use;

— Establish procedures for addressing BWC compliance concerns;

— Commit to improving international disease control and to enhance mechanisms for sending expert response teams to cope with outbreaks;

— Establish sound national oversight mechanisms for the security and genetic engineering of pathogenic organisms;

— Devise a solid framework for bioscientists in the form of a code of ethical conduct that would have universal recognition; and

— Promote responsible conduct in the study, use, modification, and shipment of pathogenic organisms.

Statement Made by the US at the Fifth BWC Review Conference

On the first day of the opening of the Fifth Review Conference, John R. Bolton, US Under Secretary of State for Arms Control and International Security, made a statement which formally presented his country's proposals[24] to strengthen the Convention. He started out with what he

---

23. Full text at http://usinfo.state.gov/topical/pol/arms/stories/01110103.htm.
24. For a comparison between the US proposals with that of the Draft Protocol, see Seth Brugger, "US Presents Alternatives to BWC Protocol at Review Conference," *Arms Control Today,* Vol. 31, no. 10, December 2001. For an analysis, see Jonathan B. Tucker and Raymond A. Zilinskas, "Assessing US proposals to Strengthen the Biological Weapons Convention," *Arms Control Today,* Vol.32, No. 3, April 2002;

thought the state parties to the BWC should do, reasons why the US rejected the draft verification protocol, and ended with the US proposals to strengthen the BWC.

Bolton said:[25]

The United States has repeatedly made clear why the arms control approaches of the past will not resolve our current problems. This is why we rejected the flawed mechanisms of the draft Protocol previously under consideration by the Ad Hoc Group. Countries that joined the BWC and then ignore their commitments and certain non-state actors would never have been hampered by the Protocol. They would not have declared their current covert offensive programmes or the locations of their illegal work nor would the draft Protocol have required them to do so. By giving proliferators the BWC stamp of approval, the Protocol would have provided them with a 'safe harbour' while lulling us into a false sense of security.

A departure from the past came when Bolton went on to say, "We also are concerned about potential use of biological weapons by terrorist groups, and states that support them. So I plan to name names. Prior to 11 September, some would have avoided this approach. The world has changed, however, and so must our business-as-usual approach." He then named the Al Qaeda, Iraq, North Korea, Iran, Libya, Syria and Sudan as a non-state actor and states of concern to the US.

Under Secretary of State's Speech in Tokyo (27 August 2002) At a briefing given at the Tokyo American Centre on 27 August 2002, Under Secretary of State for Arms Control and International Security John Bolton again spelt out the US position on the BWC. He reiterated some points and made some new ones. The crux of his speech can be found in the following para:[26]

---

25. BWC Review Conference, 19 November 2002, "US Statement to the Fifth BWC Review Conference, 19 November at http://www.acronym.org.uk/bwc/revconus.htm.
26. US Department of State, "Bolton Stresses Need to Combat Biological Weapons Threat," 27 August 2002 at: http://usinfo.state.gov/topical/pol/arms/02082702.htm.

Some have questioned the US commitment to combat the biological weapons threat due to our rejection of the draft BWC Protocol. Put simply, the Draft Protocol would have been singularly ineffective. The United States rejected the draft protocol for three reasons: first, it was based on a traditional arms control approach that will not work on biological weapons; second, it would have compromised national security and confidential business information; and third, it would have been used by proliferators to undermine other effective international export control regimes…

US Abandonment of Draft Protocol : Administration officials stated on 18 September 2002 that the draft protocol would not work and therefore, should not be salvaged.[27] Earlier, it was reported that the US was attempting to cut short the forthcoming BWC Review Conference scheduled to begin on 11 November 2002 at Geneva. Senior US diplomats attending preparatory meetings in Geneva had threatened to publicly identify suspected treaty violators unless the conference was abbreviated and discussions about the draft verification protocol avoided. They said that they would oppose any further treaty meetings until the next review conference scheduled for 2006.[28]

Statement Made by the US at Conclusion of Fifth BWC Conference

On 14 November 2002, a day before the Fifth BWC Conference formally ended, US Assistant Secretary of State for Arms Control, Stephen G. Rademaker said:[29]

We believe that the decision that has just been adopted unanimously by the conference represents a constructive and realistic work programme for the States Parties to the Biological Weapons Convention over the next three years…But it is the view of the United States that the problem of biological weapons is sufficiently grave that we cannot restrict our activities to this single forum. Our efforts to combat the threat of biological weapons have to be pressed on multiple fronts at the national level, at

27. Peter Slevin, "US Drops Bid to Strengthen Germ Warfare Accord," *The Washington Post,* 19 September 2002, p. A01.
28. David Ruppe, "BWC: With Threat, US Pressures to End Review Conference Early," *Global Security Newswire,* 6 September 2002.
29. *Available at http://www.state.gov/t/ac/ris/rm/15151.htm.*

the plurilateral level, and at the multilateral level...We believe the decision today at this Review Conference represents a realistic judgement about what can successfully be achieved in this forum over the next several years.

Other Alternative Modalities to Protocol

Alternative modalities had been proposed for the BWC meet in November 2002, also known as Review Conference Part II. Some of them are given below.

UK Green Paper. A Green Paper issued by the British government on 29 April 2002, entitled "Strengthening the Biological and Toxin Weapons Convention: Countering the Threat from Biological Weapons"[30] provides the following measures for consideration:[31]

- **Investigations** into non-compliance with the Convention (alleged use of BW, misuse of facilities and suspicious outbreaks of disease).

- **Assistance** in the event, or threat, of use of BW.

- **National criminal legislation** and extradition procedures: in those cases where they have not already done so, States Parties should pass national criminal legislation translating the prohibitions in the Convention into domestic law.

- **Scientific Advisory Panel:** in view of the dramatic pace of technical change in the life sciences as described here, an open ended body of government and non-government scientists should meet every one or two years to review the rate of change and assess their implications for the Convention and measures being taken to strengthen it.

- **Revised Confidence Building Measures (CBMs):** existing CBMs should be revisited to see whether there is scope for improving and expanding their breadth and scope. Expanded CBMs might include more detailed voluntary exchanges on the level of information as well as

30. Available at http://files.fco.gov.uk/npd/btwc290402.pdf.
31. Disarmament Documentation, "UK Green Paper on BWC, 29 April at http://www.acronym.org.uk/docs/0204/doc05.htm.

voluntary visits to be agreed between participating States Parties to facilities notified under the existing or revised CBMs, or indeed to any facilities that it was agreed could be subject to visits, reciprocal or otherwise.

- **A new Convention on Physical Protection of dangerous pathogens:** consideration should be given to the feasibility and desirability of establishing a new international agreement that would set standards for effective physical protection of dangerous pathogens held or worked upon in academic, government, industrial or research laboratories.

- **A new Convention on Criminalisation of CBW:** there are already proposals, developed initially in the academic community, for a Convention that introduces criminal responsibility for any individual indicted for violating the prohibitions in the Biological and Toxin Weapons Convention or the Chemical Weapons Convention.

- Increased efforts on **disease surveillance**, detection and diagnosis and countering infectious disease generally: this would be done through existing national and/or international channels.

- **Codes of conduct:** such codes would be developed by academic and professional bodies to lay out standards for work relevant to the prohibitions of the Convention.

- Promotion of **universal membership** of the BTWC.

- **Withdrawal of reservations to the 1925 Geneva Protocol:** States Parties to the Convention should be encouraged to withdraw any existing reservations they made on ratification or accession to the Convention regarding circumstances under which they reserved the right to use BW and CW.

Biosecurity Convention : Michel Barletta, Amy Sands and Jonathan Tucker suggested a new approach when they said that while "US officials should work with like-minded countries to develop domestic legislation to prevent unauthorised access to pathogens and to regulate germ commerce,....parallel to these efforts, the United States should promote an international biosecurity convention which would be distinct from the bioweapons treaty but would complement it by primarily addressing the threat of bioterrorism."[32]

According to the three:[33]

> The biosecurity convention should include three basic elements: a legal commitment by the contracting parties; agreed principles for developing progressively higher standards with respect to regulation and licensing of microbial culture collections; and mechanisms for oversight and progressive refinement of standards through periodic conferences. The convention would:

- Require member countries to identify microbial and toxin agents of potential concern for biowarfare and terrorism and to establish national registers of culture collections containing these agents, as well as genetically modified strains and engineered agents containing virulence factors and toxin genes transferred from the listed micro-organisms;

- Establish uniform international standards to account for and secure listed pathogens and toxins, whether they are stored, transferred, imported, or exported;

- Mandate the passage of domestic legislation to establish licensing and import/export controls over listed pathogens and toxins, and the creation of regulatory bodies to implement this system;

- Establish cooperative procedures to assist member-states in implementing the agreed safety and security standards and in establishing regulatory bodies;

- Require member states to comply fully with the convention's safety and security standards within five years of joining;

- Call for regular conferences where member states report on the development and implementation of their domestic regulatory systems

---

32. Michael Barletta, Amy Sands and Jonathan B. Tucker, "Keeping Track of Anthrax: The Case for a Biosecurity Convention," *Bulletin of the Atomic Scientists*, Vol. 58, No. 3, May/June 2002, p. 61.
33. *Ibid.*, pp. 61-62.

and answer other countries' questions regarding their compliance;

- Create a small secretariat staff in the Department of Disarmament Affairs at the United Nations to organise the review conferences and to facilitate implementation; and

- Require member-states to terminate all commerce and scientific exchanges in the field of biotechnology with any state that does not join the convention within five years of its entry into force.

Multi-pronged Approach : In another article,[34] Tucker advocated a multi-pronged approach where he suggested: measures to be taken within the framework of the BWC; national measures to strengthen the regime; and, external measures to strengthen the regime. In measures within the framework of the BWC, he advocated the strengthening of the existing CBW regime and strengthening the UN field investigation procedure. Under national measures to strengthen the regime, he suggested the criminalising of BW possession and use, and restriction of access to dangerous pathogens. Finally, under external measures to strengthening the regime, Tucker suggested the expansion of the Cooperative Threat Reduction Programme, the enhancing of global epidemiological surveillance, the encouraging of industry self-regulation, the fostering of an ethic of scientific responsibility and lastly, a provision for the oversight of hazardous research.

In a later article on the issue,[35] Jonathan Tucker, who had earlier been an arms inspector in Iraq and presently directs the Chemical and Biological Weapons Nonproliferation programme at the Monterey Institute of International Studies, called for a multilateral convention to improve security over biological agents in laboratories, which would reduce the threat of bioterrorism. He proposed a Biological Security Convention modelled on the 1994 Nuclear Safety Convention, which is an "incentive instrument" that does not enforce compliance but relies on member states

---

34. Jonathan B. Tucker, "In the Shadow of Anthrax: Strengthening the Biological Disarmament Regime," *The Nonproliferation Review,* Vol.9, No. 1, Spring 2002, pp.114-120.
35. Jonathan B. Tucker, "Preventing Terrorist Access to Dangerous Pathogens: the Need for International Biosecurity Standards," *Disarmament Diplomacy*, Issue No. 66, September 2002.

recognising the mutual benefit of nuclear safety. Since inspecting biological development facilities has proven contentious as demonstrated by the US rejection of the draft protocol to the BWC which fears that inspections might compromise legitimate military and commercial secrets without uncovering the biological weapons activities of rogue states, Tucker's convention would be a "simple document because it would lack on-site verification provisions and avoid politically contentious topics such as export controls on dual-use equipment or technology transfer." Apart from including a commitment from member parties, a set of universal controls for the "physical protection, control, licensing, and reporting of dangerous pathogens and toxins: and periodic meetings to review progress on implementing standards, the convention would require its member states to take other steps such as providing a specific list of agents of concern; establishing guidelines for registering and licensing laboratories that work with listed toxins, although a country could keep its list of such facilities confidential; conducting "personnel vetting" procedures on scientists who work with listed toxins; requiring member states to establish import and export controls and a national body to implement those controls; establishing procedures to help some member states achieve security standards and creating a small international body to organise meetings and perform administrative duties.[36]

Finally, a report published by the Stimson Center, written by eleven industry researchers and executives,[37] examines the Bush administration's alternative proposals and offers further suggestions for monitoring and implementing the convention. According to the Report, Inspectors would not have had a "fighting chance" to enforce the BWC under the proposal draft verification protocol but US-proposed alternatives to the protocol would also fall short.[38]

Conclusion : Commenting on last year's anthrax attacks, Barbara Hatch Rosenberg points out, "Paradoxically, however, by breaking the taboo

---

36. David McGlinchey, "International Response: Biological Security Convention Needed, Expert Says," *Global Security Newswire*, 27 September 2002.
37. The Henry L. Stimson Center, "Compliance Through Science: US Pharmaceutical Industry Experts on a Strengthened Bioweapons Nonproliferation Regime," Report No. 48, September 2002.
38. Ann Marie Pecha, "US Response: BWC Protocol, Proposed Alternatives Both Fall Short," *Global Security Newswire,* 1 October 2002.

on using biological weapons, the attacks have engendered a threat that could dwarf 11 September. Modes of successful attack and public response have now been demonstrated for the instruction of future terrorists."[39] It becomes all the more imperative that the BWC is strengthened with a verifying and compliance mechanism to make it a treaty with teeth.

Review Conference Part Two was crucial for deciding whether state parties are serious about giving the Convention what it sorely lacks today – a procedure that will give it a verifying and enforcing mechanism.[40] Bush administration officials had rejected the composite text outright, placed a question mark over the AHG's mandate and argued that the proposed inspection measures were ineffective as it would allow determined proliferators to conceal offensive biowarfare programmes with little risk of being caught. Additionally, officials had stated that onsite inspections would compromise the trade secrets of US pharmaceutical and biotech companies. However, the alternative measures that the US has proposed for strengthening the BWC are mostly based on domestic legislation and other voluntary actions. As pointed out, "Some of these ideas have merit, such as urging treaty members to criminalise the possession and use of bioweapons and to facilitate extradition. But others are questionable (such as the proposal for states to accept international inspections of suspicious disease outbreaks and alleged bioweapons use on a politically, not legally, binding basis), or merely in the realm of good intentions (such as devising a code of bioethics for scientists)."[41] Therefore, given that the US has agreed to further annual meetings before the Sixth Review BWC Conference scheduled for 2006 it would require a flexible approach on its part to also consider alternative proposals to strengthening the BWC regime and not stick to its intransigent stance, as at present.

---

39. Barbara Hatch Rosenberg, "Anthrax Attacks Pushed Open an Ominous Door," *Los Angeles Times*, 22 September 2002.
40. See Nicholas A. Sims, "Route-Maps to OPBW: Using the Resumed BWC Fifth Review Conference," *The CBW Conventions Bulletin*, Issue No. 56, June 2002, pp. 2-6 for Review Conference Part Two to go ahead in negotiations, with/without the Composite Text as basis for a Verification Protocol and with/without US involvement – if a majority of state members can agree on the need for a verifying and enforcing mechanism for the BWC.
41. N.32, p.60.

Tucker reminds us, "The objectives of biological disarmament are threefold: (1) to reassure law-abiding countries that potential enemies have also renounced BW; (2) to deter states that might consider acquiring BW from doing so; and (3) to contain the small number of "rogue" states, which either violate the BWC or remain outside the regime, with political, economic, or military sanctions."[42] To reemphasise the point, for the BWC to succeed as an effective treaty, it must have a verifying and enforcing mechanism. Towards this end, if the required majority of state parties believe in a multilateral approach, they must take the necessary steps for negotiations to progress, with or without the USA. Otherwise, while the countdown for the endgame to the BWC may not quite have started – it could be a startgame for it – all over again.

42. N. 33, p.112

India's Position on the BTWC and its Verification Protocol

P.R. Chari
Arpit Rajain

Introduction

Chemical and biological weapons (CBW) are sometimes called "the poor man's nuclear weapon". States that consider nuclear weapons hard to get and financially difficult to maintain have pursued CBW programmes as a second best option. Iraq's programme remains the most highlighted, but there are other countries that are suspected of having BW programmes. An inescapable reality is that some of the most plausible scenarios of WMD proliferation and their usage involve not state actors, but terrorists and other non-state actors. Obtaining and deploying biological weapons remains easy for those with enough funds and moral insensitivity. International efforts to detect and thwart such actions are constantly being challenged by advances in technologies that make detection more difficult, whilst increasing the relative ease with which biological weapons can be developed, hidden and transported.

The Biological and Toxin Weapons Convention (BTWC) is the only legal instrument that deals with the problem of biological weapons. It enjoys near universal support. As of October 2001, 145 States had signed the Convention, but 18 were yet to ratify it. Since the BTWC does not have any effective verification provisions, trust in the Convention remains largely a matter of faith, though Article VI does provide for State Parties that suspect other State Parties of non-compliance to complain to the UN Security Council. But this provision has never been invoked, and the main reason for this can be located in the intensely political nature of the Security Council itself.

The long-established Indian position on all international treaties is that they should be non-discriminatory. This position derives from its traditional disarmament diplomacy governed by adoption of a high moral posture and idealistic positions. In the words of Jawaharlal Nehru, " The objective of India is disarmament and we regard arms control as a means to achieve it...It is important to seek agreement on arms control measures, especially when we have a situation in which disarmament has become a complex problem".[1] India's statement at the time of signature provides greater insights; it declared that "India has stood for elimination of both chemical and bacteriological (biological) weapons. However, in view of the situation that developed in regard to the discussions concerning biological and chemical weapons, it became possible to reach agreement at the present moment on a Convention for the elimination of biological and toxin weapons only...The Government of India would like to reiterate in particular its understanding that the objective of the Convention is to eliminate biological and toxin weapons, thereby excluding completely the possibility of their use, and that the exemption with regard to biological agents or toxins, which would be permitted for prophylactic, protective or other peaceful purposes would not, in any way, create a loophole in regard to the production and retention of biological and toxin weapons. Also, any assistance which might be furnished under the terms of the Convention would be of medical or humanitarian nature and in conformity with the Charter of the United Nations".[2] This long citation makes clear that India, at the time when it entered the BTWC, had emphasised its disarmament aspect, and circumscribed the circumstances under which militarily useful biological agents and toxins could be produced and retained. The absence of a verification mechanism in the BTWC, of which India was aware when it signed the Convention, became a serious issue with the explosive growth of bio-technology in the 1980s. The anxiety simultaneously grew after the CWC was negotiated with stringent verification provisions, that this might create incentives for BWs to be developed by aspirant states and non-state actors.

The Protocol's History

It is common ground consequently that the absence of arrangements to verify the BTWC and ensure its compliance has greatly detracted from its worth as a non-proliferation measure. Conscious of this lacuna the Third Review Conference decided to constitute an Ad Hoc Group of Governmental Experts in September 1991 to examine what verification means are possible from a technical standpoint. This group, christened

---

1. J. P. Jain, *India and Disarmament Era,* (New Delhi: Radiant Publishers, 1974), pp.2-4.
2. India's Statement on signature available at http://www.bradford.ac.uk/acad/btwc/convention.btwcres.html accessed on 6 October 2002.

VEREX, met over 1992 and 1993 and submitted a report that was considered by a Special Conference in September 1994. It constituted an Ad Hoc Group (AHG) to draft proposals for strengthening the BTWC, and include them in a legally binding Protocol.

The AHG began working in early 1995 and intensified its activities in 1997, when a "rolling text" for a Verification Protocol was introduced to strengthen the BTWC. These deliberations were encouraged by President Clinton's exhortation in his State of the Union address in January 1998, when he declared that, " Now, we must act to prevent the use of disease as a weapon of war and terror. The Biological Weapons Convention has been in effect for 23 years. The rules are good, but the enforcement is weak and we must strengthen it with a new international system to detect and deter cheating". Following this statement the European Union evolved a Common Position committing it to concluding the negotiations and finalising the Verification Protocol. The Non-aligned Movement also committed itself to facilitating an early conclusion of the Protocol.

The essential elements of this Protocol were identified to be:

a) Mandatory Declarations of those facilities and activities of most relevance to the Convention.
b) Non-challenge visits, both focused and random, to declared facilities.
c) Both Facility and Field investigations to address a compliance concern.[3]

Additionally the elements needed for the Protocol include:

a) Measures to ensure full implementation of Article X (peaceful cooperation).
b) Measures to improve the implementation of Article IV (national implementation).
c) Measures to improve the implementation of Article III (non-transfer). [4]

---

3. Graham S. Pearson, " The Protocol to Strengthen the BWC: An Integrated Regime", Paper presented to the Pre-Meeting of the Sixth International Symposium on Protection against Chemical and Biological Warfare Agents, Stockholm, 11-15 May 1998, p. 2. *http://www.brad.ac.uk/acad/sbtwe/other/regime.htm, accessed on 30 May 2001.*

4. *Ibid.*

India's Position

Whilst discussing India's position on the BTWC and its Verification Protocol it needs initial recognition that the global concerns regarding BWs are founded on information becoming available about the extensive nature of the former Soviet BW programme, discovery of Iraq's steps to weaponise its BW inventory during the Gulf War, sarin attack by the Aum Shinrikyo sect in the Tokyo subway (1995), anthrax mail-attacks in the United States (2001-02), and, finally, evidence accumulating that Osama bin Laden was contemplating their manufacture along with chemical and radiological weapons.[5]

The confluence of these events highlighted three aspects of the BW threat. First, the notion was dispelled that the use of biological weapons is unthinkable. Indeed, non-state actors belonging to the genre of religious terrorists could use them as weapons of choice to inflict an apocryphal vengeance on their victims. Second, India has also endured anthrax mail-attacks. Several of them were hoaxes, but the alarm and disruption caused was considerable, which was probably the true intention of the attackers. Third, Osama bin Laden has identified India, apart from the United States and Israel, as his chief enemy. The joint effect of all these developments has been to heighten awareness in public consciousness of a possible BW attack. For its part, India joined the United States in identifying international terrorism as being the major threat to its security, which includes the CBW threat from terrorists acting in concert with states that are inimical to India.[6]

The Indian approach to the various issues in contention during the negotiations to finalise the Verification Protocol can now be considered. But it should initially be pointed out that they have only a historical value now, since the AHG was dismantled in November 2001; hence the future of the Verification Protocol is currently in limbo. Of a possible BW attack five issues that were in dispute would be discussed below. They provide an insight into India's position on these questions pertaining to verifying the BTWC.

a) **Reconciling Articles III and X:** Article III embodies the regulatory principle in the BTWC; it prohibits the transfer "to any recipient

---

5. See chapter on *Bioterrorism and the Future,* in this volume for more details.
6. " Bin Laden's Group has Deadly Weapons", *The Indian Express,* 20 April 1999.

whatsoever, directly or indirectly, and not in any way to assist, encourage, or induce any State, group of States or international organisations to manufacture or otherwise acquire any of the agents, toxins, weapons, equipment or means of delivery specified in Article I of the Convention." However, Article I permits trade in biological agents and toxins that are 'dual-purpose' in nature for medical, agricultural and other developmental purposes. This article does not include non-state actors since this was not envisaged when the BTWC was enacted, which is especially disconcerting after 9/11 drew attention to the likelihood of bioterrorism becoming the new threat to international security. A system of export controls is, therefore, needed, which must be supplemented by strong national implementation measures to ensure that the prohibitions of the BTWC are enforced. At the same time, the development promise in Article X cannot be ignored, which adumbrates that the State Parties are obliged to facilitate, and have the right to participate in the fullest possible exchange of equipment, materials and scientific and technological information for peaceful purposes. A balance of rights and obligations between the State Parties was thus established in the BTWC by balancing the prohibitions of Article III against the developmental aspect of Article X. It is generally believed that access to new biotechnologies has decreased since it came into force in 1975 due to the increasingly stringent protection of proprietary information. Consequently, control over dual-purpose items and technologies, though imperative to serve the ends of checking the proliferation of biological agents and toxins, should not affect the need for promoting bio-technology for developmental purposes.

Effecting this reconciliation by negotiating the establishment of guiding principles lay at the heart of the Verification Protocol to the BTWC. The required dual approach was incorporated into a Working Paper submitted by India to the Ad Hoc Group in March 1997. It proposed strengthening the implementation of Article X by making equipment and technologies developed by a State participating in the compliance regime available for biological defence, collaborative research and development projects, joint ventures for biological defence, including development of vaccines and diagnostic systems, and transfers of technology for peaceful use in genetic engineering and biotechnology.[7] Simultaneously, India accepted the need for " strengthened implementation of the provisions of Article III [to] ensure that the cooperation envisaged under Article X is not abused."[8] The guidelines suggested by India to regulate transfers of dual-use agents and equipment envisaged declarations being made by the recipient to the exporting country providing information about the purpose of the transfer, the source of the items, quantity required, final destination, intended use, and an end-use certificate, along with information regarding secondary transfers, if applicable.[9] The centrality of a balanced approach towards the provisions of the Convention was emphasised in another Working Paper that India joined by suggesting, "a mechanism should be established to deal with the issue of settlement of disputes of transfer denial".[10]

b) **Commitment to Transparency:** The most contentious issue before the Ad Hoc Group was on-site inspections to ensure that the verification process acquires some credibility. Declarations are essential to obtain basic information on facilities that could possess BW capabilities. This needs to be supplemented by a system of facility and field investigations, either in the routine, or expressly designed to investigate suspicious activities. Except for declarations that were accepted, the issues of "non-challenge" or "random" visits, but more so, "challenge" inspections became matters of major controversy in the Ad Hoc Group. India's broad approach to these issues was to ensure a reasonable degree of transparency, including on-site verification measures, without compromising either proprietary information or national security interests. There is particular sensitivity, however, to field visits for investigating outbreaks of disease, given the undeniable fact

---

7. Working Paper by India, Measures to Strengthen Implementation of Article X of the BTWC, *BWC/ Ad Hoc Group/ WP, 131,* 10 March 1997.
8. *Ibid.*
9. BWC Ad Hoc Group, *Rolling Text of a Protocol to the Convention on the Prohibition of the Development, Production and Stockpiling of Biological and Toxin Weapons and on Their Destruction,* 30 July 1997, pp. 29-30.
10. Cf. Working paper by China, Cuba, India, Indonesia, Islamic Republic of Iran, Libyan Arab Jamahariya, Pakistan and Sri Lanka, Geneva, 19 November-7 December 2001 on "Transfer of Equipment and Biological Materials for Peaceful Application," *BWC/CONF.V/COW/WP.25* dated 27 November 2001.

that India suffers from frequent epidemics reflecting the poor state of public hygiene in the country. There is also sensitivity to on-site inspections becoming instruments of harassment. India's further positions on these matters were elucidated as follows:

1. It joined Indonesia and Mexico in proposing to the Ad Hoc Group that requests for dual-use items and technologies should be accompanied by detailed information regarding their intended purpose, location of the facility requesting them, and end-use certification.[11] India supports a verification regime that requires declarations, and had suggested that this could be achieved in four formats relating to past and present bio-offence facilities, past bio-defence facilities, and other related activities.[12] In theory, strong rules of disclosure would ensure that, "documenting compliance with these standards would provide continuous positive reassurances that relevant activities were being safely managed and exclusively devoted to legitimate purposes".[13]
2. A system solely dependent on declarations would not, obviously, be satisfactory without a mechanism to physically check their veracity. Besides clarifying the contents of declarations, these checks were useful to familiarise inspectors with sensitive facilities. Despite its initial scepticism about their worth, India was not opposed to such inspections/ visits, provided a prior consultation process was established.[14] These "non-challenge" inspections or "random" visits became controversial with the United States opposing them due to the opposition of its pharmaceutical and biotechnology industry; they wished

---

11. Working Paper by India, Indonesia and Mexico: Measures to Strengthen the Implementation of Article III of the Biological and Toxin Weapons Convention, *BWC/Ad Hoc Group/WP. 232*, 3 October 1997.
12. *BWC/ Ad Hoc Group/ WP. 318,* 30 September 1998.
13. John D. Steinbruner, "Biological Weapons: A Plague Upon All Houses", *Foreign Policy,* No. 109, Winter 1997-98, p. 93.
14. P. R. Chari land Giri Deshingkar, "Putting Teeth into the BWC: An Indian View", in Susan Wright, Richard Falk (eds) Symposium: Biological Warfare, Responding to the Challenge of Biological Warfare—A Matter of Contending Paradigms of Thought and Action: Introduction, *Politics and the Life Sciences,* March 1999, p. 89.

that such visits would only be undertaken in a circumscribed manner to clarify specific ambiguities in the declarations made. The compromise suggested by the UK envisaged "transparency visits" in the nature of " briefing tours", apart from randomly selected visits. India's concerns were especially focused on the possibility of clarification " visits" turning into " investigations". Some part of these concerns were occasioned by the need to protect sensitive commercial proprietary information and legitimate national security concerns".[15] It, therefore, joined the NAM group to suggest that State Parties might initiate visits for clarification purposes, which was added to the Rolling Text.[16]

3. In contrast to the voluntary nature of " non-challenge" or "random" visits, an element of involuntariness was associated with "challenge" inspections that are intended to investigate suspect facilities or suspicious outbreaks of disease or detect undeclared facilities. There was some dispute among BWC adherents about the mechanism to launch a "challenge" inspection. The United States wanted three-fourths of the State Parties to approve a challenge inspection ("green light" procedure), which would have been very difficult to obtain. Other countries wanted a "red light" procedure whereby three-fourths of the State Parties were required to vote for stopping a " challenge" inspection from proceeding ahead, which would enable its easier execution. India favoured the "green light" procedure with the qualification that decisions to challenge inspections would have to be taken within a specified time frame.[17] It was also assumed that all such decisions would be taken by an Executive Council elected by the State Parties joining the Protocol.

c) ***Definitions:*** The operative clause of the BTWC, Article I, enjoins State Parties not to develop, produce, stockpile or otherwise

15. Government of India, Ministry of External Affairs, *Annual Report 1997-98,* p. 92.
16. BWC Ad Hoc Group, NAM and Other States, Working Paper: "Proposed" Text for Visits, UN Document *BWC Ad Hoc Group/ WP.402,* 22 September 1999.
17. P.R. Chari and Giri Deshingkar, "Putting Teeth into the BWC", p. 89, citing interviews with officials in the Ministry of External Affairs.

acquire or retain: microbial or other biological agents or toxins whatever their origin or method of production, of types and in quantities that have no justification for prophylactic, protective or other peaceful purposes". Strangely, the word "use" does not occur in this clause. Terms like "biological agent", moreover, are very broad and imprecise. The basic objective of the BTWC is to eliminate a whole class of weapons of mass destruction. The controversy was therefore focused on whether such terms should be clearly defined to ensure that discretion does not pass into the hands of the inspectors (Russian position) or left vague to allow incorporation of new and genetically engineered agents that make the finalising of precise lists futile (American position). Laying down quantitative restrictions would be equally futile, because cultures can be quickly grown into militarily useful amounts (American position). A via media solution suggested was to write out definitions for terms that were essential for a verification regime, and only for the purpose of implementing the Protocol.[18] India has not taken sides in this controversy, but appreciates the links between definitions and declarations; hence it wants the definitions to apply to the entire Protocol, rather than parts thereof. Further, it was officially stated that Article I " cannot be constrained by the state of scientific and technological knowledge at a particular point of time and should be interpreted to take into account any further developments in science and technology which can be seen to be in violation of the general prohibitions contained in the article. Today, this would include advances in the area of genome sequencing and advances in the modification of toxins and bio-regulators".[19] India also favoured the word " use" being included in Article I.

d) ***Organisation:*** Initially India favoured the establishment of a Secretariat that would be "small and cost effective and [which] should be in a position to utilise existing networks of information

---

18. Susan Wright, "Cuba Case Tests Treaty", *The Bulletin of the Atomic Scientists,* November/ December 1997, p. 19.
19. Arundhati Ghose, *Statement,* Fourth Review Conference of the State Parties to the Convention on the Prohibition of the Development, Production and Stockpiling of Bacteriological (Biological) and Toxin Weapons and on their Destruction, 26 November 1996, p. 4.

such as those of the WHO".[20] Later, it joined the Non-Aligned group in opting for a more democratic body than the Security Council comprising a small body of BTWC adherents to guide its actions and to take decisions on urgent matters. A rival proposal envisaged a specialised organisation being established on the lines of the OPCW that would enable declarations to be checked, challenge inspections effected, and "non-challenge" visits to be routinely undertaken.[21]

e) ***Confidentiality of Proprietary Information:*** It has been my contention that India has traditionally straddled the developed and developing countries in shaping its policy approaches towards the Verification Protocol. Briefly, both its commercial and security interests have shaped India's positions towards the confidentiality issue. The influence of its growing pharmaceutical and biotechnology industry, apart from its scientific establishment, has shaped its commercial interests. This becomes clear from India's declaration that: " Concerning a compliance Protocol in (sic) the BTWC, India maintains that this should be formulated and implemented in a manner which protects sensitive commercial proprietary information and legitimate national security considerations. The verification measures should be non-discriminatory and avoid any negative impact on scientific research, international cooperation and industrial development".[22]

Conclusion

The foregoing informs us about India's basic approaches towards the issues in contention for negotiating a Verification Protocol to the BTWC. The significance of verification cannot be underestimated in the light of recent infractions of the BTWC by its signatories (Russia, Iraq) and the misdeeds of non-state actors (Aum Shinrikyo). Currently, the BTWC is the only arms control agreement that has no provisions for its verification. India has vigorously participated in the long negotiations held in the Ad Hoc Group. It also chaired the sub-group on national implementation

---

20. *Op. cit.,* p. 5.
21. Malcolm Dando, "Strengthening the Biological Weapons Convention: Moving towards the Endgame," *Disarmament Diplomacy,* 21 December 1997, p. 13.
22. Ministry of External Affairs, *Annual Report 1997-98*, p. 92.

and commitment, one of eight sub-groups formed to address the specific issues that surfaced during the negotiations. Its dual concerns can be summarised in its expectation that "The negotiations should yield a strengthened BTWC which not only ensures effective verification of elimination of yet another class of weapons of mass destruction but also facilitates the transfer and exchange of biotechnology for peaceful purposes".[23] Hence India involved itself deeply in discussions with non-Western countries, along with China and South Africa, to evolve a modus vivendi and seek compromise solutions for the many issues in contention. This should belie any doubts that India was indifferent to the finalisation of a Verification Protocol to the BTWC.

India's basic position towards the Verification Protocol was reiterated at the Fifth Review Conference (November 2001) emphasising that, "The promotional aspects of Article X are, we believe, a crucial element in strengthening the convention and even perhaps in achieving universal adherence".[24] It was also pointed out that the moral and legal norms embodied in the BTWC required strengthening, both nationally and multilaterally. A three-fold strategy was envisaged comprising, "First, the norm of prohibition of BW embodied in the BWC, needs to be strengthened and this is where the Protocol, in accordance with the 1994 mandate, becomes a crucial input. Secondly, recent incidents have also highlighted the need for enhanced national controls on production, acquisition, storage, handling, transfer and uses of dangerous pathogens. Some of these controls already exist in the form of international guidelines; what is needed is sensitisation and widespread adherence. Finally, international cooperation and assistance is not only necessary for dealing with use or threat of use of biological weapons but reflects the political commitment of the international community to deal with such threat in a collective fashion. In fact, cooperation between States should become all the more networked to prevent non-state actors from exploiting gaps in it".[25]

India had expressed its apprehensions when the US expressed its doubts

---

23 *Ibid.*

24. Rakesh Sood, *Statement*, 20 November 2001, Fifth Review Conference of the States Parties to the Convention on the Prohibition of the Development, Production and Stockpiling of Bacteriological (Biological) and Toxin Weapons and their Destruction.

25. *Ibid.*

in May 2001 and its rejection of the Verification Protocol in July 2001. This was prior to the 9/11 events and the Fifth Review Conference. Finally, the United States also rejected both the Rolling Text and the Chairman's 'Composite Text', which effectively annulled the achievements of this six-year long exercise,[26] by proposing on the last day of the Conference that the Ad Hoc Group should be suspended, and that the conference should hold annual meetings, starting in November 2002 to "consider and assess progress by State Parties in implementing the new measures adopted at the Fifth Review Conference" and to " consider new measures or mechanisms for effectively strengthening the BWC". In exchange for its continued participation in these negotiations the US demanded the termination of the Ad Hoc Group's mandate. Coerced in this manner the State Parties decided to adjourn the Conference for one year as a "cooling off" period. The effect of this postponement was to ensure the demise of the AHG and the Verification Protocol.

The new US strategy to counter BW proliferation will apparently be founded on " tightened export controls, intensified non-proliferation dialogue, increased domestic preparedness and controls, enhanced biodefense and counterterrorism capabilities, and innovative measures against disease outbreaks, as well as the full compliance by all State Parties with the global ban".[27] The adjourned Review Conference is scheduled to reconvene on 11 November 2002 to resume its deliberations. The prognosis is not propitious for its success with the US claiming that the present Convention will not work and should not be salvaged; instead, discussions should be postponed till 2006.[28] The irony in this situation cannot be overstated; just when the need for strengthening the BTWC has become imperative due to the assaults upon it by state and non-State actors, the United States has effectively disrupted the finalisation of a much-needed verification regime to provide teeth to the BTWC.

---

26. Jenni Rissanen, "Anger After the Ambush: Review Conference Suspended After US Asks for AHG's Termination", *BWC Conference Bulletin,* The Acronym Institute, 9 December 2001.
27. Fact Sheet, "The Biological Weapons Convention", US Department of State, Bureau of Arms Control, 22 May 2002, *http://usembassy.state.gov/delhi.html,* p. 1.
28. Peter Slevin, "US Drops Bid to Strengthen Germ Warfare Accord", *Washington Post,* 19 September 2002.

What will be India's position at the resumed Review Conference? This can be inferred from the Government's answers to Parliament Questions seeking information on its stand regarding the US role in winding up the Ad Hoc Group. In measured terms, Parliament was informed that, " India supports efforts aimed at strengthening the BTWC. India along with the Non-aligned Movement (NAM) has regretted the rejection of the Draft Protocol. NAM has also emphasised the continued validity of the mandate given to the Ad hoc Group, and underlined that the BTWC needs to be strengthened through a non-discriminatory legally-binding instrument to be negotiated multilaterally within the framework of the Convention".[29]

A careful reading of this answer makes clear that India would, most probably, join the NAM in exploring other options on the assumption that reviving the Draft Verification Protocol is unrealistic. It seems unlikely that India will make an issue of it, should the United States continue to oppose negotiations on reviving the Verification Protocol on the pragmatic consideration that any verification arrangements devised for the BTWC would be meaningless in the absence of the United States. What other options are discovered in Geneva, in place of the defunct Verification Protocol, to verify that State Parties are adhering by the BTWC, remains to be seen, because the issues and the problems associated with verifying the BTWC continue unchanged.

---

29. Unstarred Question No. 3900 answered on 2 May 2002, *http://www.meadev.nic.in/govt/parl-qa/rajyasabha/may2-3900.htm, on 3 August 2002.*

Threat Analysis of Danger from Biological Weapons and Biodefence Measures

Maj. Gen. Ashok Krishna, AVSM (Retd.)

Introduction

Biological weapons present a multifaceted threat. We should not just be concerned about the use of such weapons for bioterrorism, assassination or economic warfare against staple crops, but also for tactical or strategic military use on the battlefield, and as weapons of mass destruction. Moreover, the different types of weapon agents bacteria, toxins, viruses, bio-regulators can each cause different disease symptoms that require detection and recognition prior to treatment.

Biological weapons present a rapidly growing threat because of the current revolution in biotechnology being brought about by the Human Genome Project (HPG). Hence, anxieties in this regard cannot be lightly dismissed. This article is concerned with the threat that biological weapons pose, and the defensive measures possible against them.

The Threat of Biological Weapons

It is often said that nuclear weapons are a deterrent and are not meant for use. The same could be said of biological weapons though with some reservations. Biological weapons are called the poor man's weapon; hence, their use by individuals, terrorists, non-state actors[1] and even states is more plausible than the use of nuclear weapons, because these weapons have been used before and their development continues apace. Therefore states must evolve concepts and doctrines to counter them effectively, should they be used by terrorists or on the battlefield.

The classical biological agents—such as anthrax botulinium toxins (BTX)— remain the primary concern today because they would not require

1. Till date there has not been a single successful biological weapons attack by terrorists: Walter Laquer, *The New Terrorism* (London: Phoenix,1999), p.67. The author has discussed the history and future of germ warfare: pp. 61-70.

testing by a large-scale proliferator. This is quite apparent from agents chosen to be weaponised in Iraq's offensive biological weapons programme. We also know that the Soviet Union's huge offensive biological weapons programme used genetic engineering techniques to make specific modifications, to agents. It may be possible, for example, to improve the environmental resistance of agents or to modify a benign micro-organism so that it produces a damaging toxin. Such specific modifications, especially if used in combination, could make these dangerous agents more usable on the battlefield or for terrorist purposes.

The Chemical and Biological Weapons Spectrum

Chemical and biological weapons are best considered together as forming a threat spectrum as under:-

(a) Chemical.
   (i) Classical chemical weapons: mustard gas, nerve gas.
   (ii) Emerging chemical weapons: toxic industrial chemicals, toxic pharmaceutical chemicals, toxic agricultural chemicals.

(b) Chemicals of biological origin.
   (i) Bio-regulators: peptides.
   (ii) Toxins: sanitoxin, mycotoxin, ricin.

(c) Biological organisms.
   (i) Genetically manipulated biological weapons: modified/tailored bacteria, viruses.
   (ii) Traditional biological weapons: bacteria, viruses, rickettsia.

Between classical man made chemical agents such as nerve gas at one end, and traditional, naturally occurring living biological agents anthrax bacteria at the other, there is some overlap in the group of naturally occurring chemicals produced by biological organisms. These so-called mid-spectrum agents—bio-regulators and toxins—are important biological weapons. Toxins and bio-regulators have a history of misuse. One well-known example of the use of ricin was in the killing of the Bulgarian dissident Georgi Markov in London in 1978.While walking in London, Markov was jabbed in the thigh by the tip of an umbrella. Unknown to doctors treating him, a small metal pellet containing ricin, was left in the muscle. He died a few days later from the effects of that poison.

The biotechnology revolution will engender a profound change in our understanding of how the human nervous system and associated endocrine and immune systems work, in which chemical messengers play a very important role. Misuse of this new neuro-science could provide a novel means of manipulating human behaviour by chemical means. In examining potential misuse of combinations of advances from different scientific fields, possible ethnic targeting of toxins and bio-regulators could be an extreme case.[2]

Range of BW Agents

An official 1992 French paper prepared to consider whether the Biological and Toxin Weapons Convention , could be verified, set out the range of agents covered by the convention as follows:-

(a) Living agents capable of self- reproduction: bacteria, fungi, etc.

(b) Living agents capable of reproduction only in a host cell: viruses.

(c) Non-living agents incapable of reproduction, but secreted by living organisms: peptides, toxins.

(d) Non-living agents incapable of reproduction that are obtained by chemical synthesis, but whose structure is identical or very similar to that of agents mentioned in (c) above.[3]

Thus a bacterium like anthrax is able to infect a host organism and reproduce inside that host. A virus such as smallpox, however, not only has to infect a host organism but also enter the cells of that organism to subvert the cell's machinery to reproduce itself. Agents such as toxins cannot reproduce; they are non-living chemicals either secreted by living organisms or synthesised by scientists. A proliferator seeking biological weapons, therefore, has a wide range of agents to choose from. The ideal agent would possess certain characteristics such as ease of production and storage, robustness on dispersal, and a predictable effect on the

---

2. Malcolm Dando, *The New Biological Weapons* (London: Boulder, 2001), p.p. 10-12.
3. *Ibid.*, p. 18.

intended victims. One possible disadvantage of biological agents such as bacteria and viruses is that, after initial infection, there is a certain time lag before they multiply and cause illness. Should a more rapid effect be required, a toxin might be used because it could be expected to act more rapidly. This would be particularly true if the toxin is used in the most effective way, that is, dispersed in large quantities by wind and inhaled directly into the lungs of the intended victims. Not surprisingly, therefore, the classical biological agents weaponised by the US included two toxic weapons: botulinum toxin and staphylococcal enterotoxin B (SEB). Botulinum toxin is among the most deadly substances known to humans, whereas staphylococcal B would incapacitate most victims for days. Hence, these toxins indicate the range of possibilities open to weapons designers.[4]

Bio-regulatory and Toxin Weapons

Bio-regulatory Weapons : Bio-regulators are natural substances produced in very small quantities that are essential for the normal physiological functioning of the body. They control cell and physiological functions and regulate a broad range of functions, such as bronco-constriction, vasodilation, muscle contraction, blood pressure, heart rate, temperature and immune responses. These substances can be harmful in large concentrations or if modifications to them bring about changes in the nature and duration of their action. Exploited in such a way for military purposes, they could potentially cause such effects as rapid unconsciousness, heart failure, paralysis, hypotension or hypertension, or psychological disturbances. These substances exert their effects in the fraction of a second, and comparatively, very small quantities are required.

By means of modern genetic engineering, it is possible to allow bacteria or viruses to produce the substances on a large scale or to use micro-organisms to spread these substances to humans, plants or animals. Bio-regulatory agents have long been of interest to the military, both for attacking plants and human beings. What has clearly happened in recent years is that many more of these substances have been discovered.

---

4. Office of the Secretary of Defence, USA, *Proliferation Threat and Response,* January 2001, p.p. 113-114.

ToxinWeapons : A toxin is a substance that should:-

(a) Be a substance of natural occurrence (plant, animal, bacteria, etc.).
(b) Be foreign to the victim.
(c) Be predominantly toxic and adverse to the well-being or life of the victim.

These complexities are best illustrated by the example of histamine in wasp venom introduced into a human being through a sting. Although histamine occurs naturally in humans, the histamine from the sting is considered a toxin because it is applied in a toxic dose under unusual conditions. Similarly, digitoxin, the active ingredient in digitalis poisoning would be considered a toxin even though it might be used for therapeutic purposes, such as treating heart disease.

On the other hand, a bio-regulator which is a naturally occurring constituent of a victim's body could be misused to damage health or cause death by introducing unnatural quantities into the body. A weapons designer might find it possible to attack by disrupting such natural bio-regulatory systems—for example, by vastly increasing the concentration within the living organism of a naturally occurring bio-regulatory chemical, or by introducing large quantities of a substance that mimics its effects.[5]

Biological weapons were developed in the offensive programmes of major states for use against humans, animals and plants. It is in attacks on plants that the use in warfare of bio-regulatory mimics on a massive scale has been demonstrated. In a major study, *The Problem of Chemical and Biological Warfare* (from SIPRI), it was reported in 1970:-

"Chemical anti-plant agents [mimics] began to attract military interest at the time of World War II but it was not until US involvement in Vietnam that they came to be employed on a significant scale in combat. Here they were used either to defoliate vegetation, thus removing natural cover that might conceal the enemy, or to destroy food crops."
To give an example, US herbicide usage by type of mission in Vietnam

---

5. Malcolm Dando, N.2, p.p.17-32.

was as under:-

<u>Usage in thousands of litres</u>[6]

	Agent Orange	Agent White	Agent Blue
Forest and vegetation	40,525	19,623	1,996
Crop	3,813	212	6,185
Total	44,338	19,835	8,182

Note: To convert volume data to area coverage in hectares, multiply by 35.6.

Classical BW agents pose the greatest concern for the near and the mid-term. Iraq's biological weapons programme[7] illustrates that there was considerable advantage for a proliferator in going first for agents such as anthrax botulinum toxin, known to have been successfully weaponised in the past. The engineering problems would be known and testing problems would be considerably reduced. Iraq produced 19,000 litres of botulinium toxin and some of it was weaponised in 100 botulinum bombs and 16 missile warheads. Iraq claims to have destroyed these weapons is not being accepted pending fresh weapons' inspections.

Emerging Trends

The current level of sophistication of many biological agents is low, but there is enormous potential — based on advances in modern molecular biology, fermentation and drug delivery technology — for making more sophisticated weapons. While historically it has been possible to alter the characteristics of biological weapon agents, making one change by ordinary methods often produced a second change — detrimental and unwanted — in the agent's characteristics. Now, however, advances in biotechnology, genetic engineering and related sciences provide increasing potential to control these factors, possibly leading to the ability to use biological warfare agents as tactical battlefield weapons. A new set of agents that might be produced by genetic engineering are:-[8]

(a) Benign micro-organisms, genetically altered to produce a toxin, venom or bio-regulator.

---

6. *Ibid.* p., 27.
7. Josh Tyrangiel, "What Saddam's Got," *Time*, 13 May 2002, p.p.1.30-31.
8. W. S. Cohen, *Proliferation Threat and Response(1997),* Technical Annex available on line at http://www.defenselink.mil/pubs/prolif97/annex.html

(b) Micro-organisms resistant to antibiotics, standard vaccines and therapeutics.

(c) Micro-organisms with enhanced aerosol and environmental stability.

(d) Immunology altered micro-organisms able to defeat standard identification, detection and diagnostic methods.

(e) Combination of the above four types with improved delivery systems.

Four technological trends are likely to influence the likelihood of new agents being developed:-

(a) Genetically engineered vectors in the form of modified infectious organisms will be increasingly employed as tools in medicine as they become more widely available.

(b) Strides will be made in understanding infectious disease mechanisms and microbial genetics that are responsible for disease processes.

(c) An increased understanding of the human immune system, function and disease mechanisms will shed light on the circumstances that cause individual susceptibility to infectious diseases.

(d) Vaccines and antidotes will be improved over the long term, perhaps to the point where classical biological warfare agents will be less useful as a means of causing casualties.

Cell Receptors: Receptors are proteins made up of long chains of different amino acids.[9] The 20 amino acids commonly found in the human body have different structures; thus changes in the sequence of amino acids

9. Malcolm Dando, N.2, p.p. 87-100.

in a receptor will change the overall structure of the receptor because the protein will take on a different final shape. As human knowledge about cell receptors increases, it will be possible to potentially interfere with their operation for both benign purposes (when they malfunction in disease) or for malign purposes to construct new biological weapons.

It may well be asked if bio-regulators and toxins are chemicals and are therefore covered by the Chemical Weapons Convention, should there be any concern about their potential misuse? Yes indeed, because the convention has apparently not eliminated the search for new and more effective chemical and biological agents and there is an overlap between these two types of agents.

Agent Delivery

Aerosol Dissemination: State sponsored biological warfare programmes have concentrated on agents that can be delivered through the air, either when released from an exploding munition or an aerosol cloud generated by a sprayer. The potential threat from aerosol clouds according to a World Health Organisation estimate is that, 50 kilograms of dry anthrax used against a city of one million people would kill 36,000 people and incapacitate another 54,000.[10] For strategic purposes, remotely piloted vehicles, long-range fighter bombers, or cruise missiles equipped with tanks and sprayers could disperse agents under atmosphere conditions favourable for carrying out such an attack. For tactical use, agents could be delivered by rockets and artillery shells. Technology needed for aerosol dissemination is commercially available. Terrorist groups have hitherto not attempted to master this technology.

Water : Water systems have been targeted by terrorist groups, but they are less vulnerable than often imagined. Municipal water systems are designed to eliminate impurities, especially pathogens, to protect public health. As part of this process, communities filter water to remove harmful organisms and add chlorine to kill those remaining. Although extremely

---

10. W. Seth Carus, "The Threat of Bioterrorism," *The Indian Defence Review,* Vol 13(1), January-March 1998, p.p. 40-43.

difficult, there have been several attempts to deliberately contaminate water supplies with biological agents.

Food: Adversaries have tried to contaminate food. In general only uncooked or improperly stored food is vulnerable to biological agents, since the heat generated during cooking destroys most pathogens and toxins. This implies that foods that are commonly eaten uncooked, or are contaminated after being cooked would have to be targeted. Alternatively, reliance would have to be placed on a toxin that can survive cooking.

Anti-Agriculture: Biological agents can be used against agricultural targets. Iraq admits that during the 1980s it was developing at least one biological agent for use against crops, including wheat smut rust, which makes infected grain unusable for human consumption.

Drug Delivery: Pharmaceutical companies are trying to devise new methods of drug induction other than intake by oral means or by injection.. One way of introducing chemicals into the body is by inhalation into the lungs. What is now happening is an across-the-board range of developments in capabilities for the delivery of drugs by inhalation. This cannot but have implications for the possibility of delivery of toxins or peptides for malignant purposes also.

Dimensions and Types of Biological Warfare (BW)

The dimensions of BW are best described in terms of the nature of the aggressor, the scale of release of the agent, and the target. Within each of these dimensions there could be three prominent divisions:-

(a) Nature of the Aggressor. Nations, sub-national groups, and individuals.

(b) Scale of Release of the Agent. Point source release, medium scale release, and large-scale release.

(c) Target. Humans, plants, animals.

If we see humans to be the target of attack, then there are nine possible types of BW, ranging from a point source criminal act by an individual to a large-scale military strategic act by a state:-[11]

Scale of Release	Nature of Aggressor		
of the Agent	Individual	Subnational Group	State
Point source	Criminal act	Assassination	Assassination
Medium scale	Criminal act	Terrorist act	Military tactical
Large scale	Not possible	National liberation	Military strategic (army) use

As nuclear weapons are not likely to be the choice for non-state terrorist groups, an aggrieved group that decides to kill large numbers of innocent people—to instil confusion and fear—will find its mission easier to accomplish with anthrax. Thousands of scientists and technicians are busy today designing and producing weapons loaded with deadly microbes. They are not confined to some countries of the developing world, but include the US, Russia, China and others. They carry out research and development with the stated purpose of developing a range of measures to counter bioweapons.[12]

Agent Selection

Against this background, we can ask where toxins, bio-regulators and other agents might fit into the thinking about operational planning for biological warfare. To be effective in war, bacterial agents should be able to meet certain requirements. Broadly speaking they should produce casualties, infect easily and spread quickly, survive in unfavourable conditions, be available in quantity and be difficult to detect. The use of any particular agent—germ or poison—would depend largely on what is hoped to be accomplished.[13] For example:-

(a) If the intention is to kill a large number of people then germs of cholera, plague, small-pox and typhus, which can spread rapidly, may be used.

---

11. Malcolm Dando, N.2, p. 122.
12. Lt. Gen. R. K. Jasbir Singh (ed), *Indian Defence Yearbook 2002*, Chapter 5.
13. Based on *Amplification Notes to Chemical and Biological Warfare Manual* issued by the Defence Services Staff College, Wellington, 1981.

(b) However, if the intention is to incapacitate as many people as possible, with a view to demoralising them, causing shortages in production, reduction of combat efficiency and tying up of doctors and hospitals, then biological agents with low mortality may be used. In this case, spread of diseases like rabbit fever, malaria and influenza would achieve the desired results.

(c) On the other hand, when the intention is to reduce food supplies, BWs can be directed primarily against livestock, poultry and food crops. Diseases such as anthrax, glanders and rinder-pest, can be aimed against livestock. In the case of poultry, fowl plague and the so-called "Newcastle disease" would be successful. Against food crops, all kinds of plant plagues and blights may be employed. For greater effect, bio-regulators could be used to destroy food plants.

Whatever germs, poisons or other BW agents are employed, their effectiveness would be dependent on suitable atmospheric conditions in which to thrive; susceptibility of the objective to the disease being spread; and measures to prevent the attacker from being infected himself. Unless these conditions are fulfilled to the satisfaction of the attacker, BW cannot be waged successfully. These conditions cannot always be fulfilled. Further, almost all BW agents are susceptible to the environment and can thrive only with proper moisture, food, light and temperature. They are easily destroyed by boiling or chlorinating water, by cooking food, and by exposure to sunlight. The use of soap and water also destroys them.

Agricultural Warfare.[14] During the Cold War, the United States not only used synthetic plant *auxins* to attack vegetation in Vietnam but also did careful planning for destruction of the staple food crops of the enemy. The agents of choice, 4-flourophenoxyacetic acid (KF) and related compounds, were effective against cereal spices at about the same level of application as agents like 2, 4-D and 2,4,5,-T were against broad leaf plants. Additionally, if used alone against rice at certain stages of its development, the agent had no discernible effect for some time. Only when the rice plants approached maturity did it become apparent that the

---

14. S. Whitby and P. R. Rogers, Anti- crop Biological Warfare: Implications of the Iraqi and US Programmes, *Defence Analysis* vol.13, No 3, p.p. 303-318.

grains were not filling out. Extensive studies were carried out on rice plants to cover all relevant aspects and it was found that, at the recommended use rate of 0.5 pounds per acre applied during the susceptible period of rice, the yield may be reduced by 50 to 100 per cent. Thus, a loss of 336 to 672 metric tons of rice per square mile could be expected. The report recommended that because of its potential, the capability to wage anti-rice warfare was desirable.

Using Toxin Weapons : In general terms, biological weapons like toxins and bio-regulators share the potential with all chemicals and biological weapons for causing extreme psychological stress in response to their use, because of the unfamiliarity of the threat they pose. This would apply as much to the use of bio-regulators of a less lethal kind as to highly lethal toxins. The speed of action of these chemical toxins and bio-regulators as opposed to the relative slowness of action of live pathogens—requiring multiplication of the infective agent in the victim prior to its exerting an effect—would argue for the potential use of toxins and bio-regulators where a speedy result is required.

Ethnic Weapons : An attack on a particular ethnic group using biological weapons need not be a sophisticated attack. It could be as crude as using a toxin weapon on an ethnic group. Iraq was interested in *aflatoxin* as a means of causing long term damage to its Kurdish population by mixing the toxin with riot control agents. The intent of the assault would not be detectable until decades later when large numbers of people would begin to develop liver cancer. Another crude method of assault would be to use a toxin against which its own troops had been vaccinated but the victims had not.

Offensive Aspects of BW

Though untried so far in any war, due consideration must be paid to the moral and political effects of BW. At present, it is more likely to be used as a strategic weapon rather than as a tactical one because of the time lag before the effects are apparent.[15] Its tactical employment could be as follows:-

---

15. *Manual on Chemical and Biological Warfare* issued by the Infantry School, Mhow.1993.

(a) **Close fighting:** This is only feasible if attacking troops are immunised.

(b) **Against isolated targets:** Such as naval bases, islands and isolated nodes. For example, Malta would have been a suitable target during the Second World War II.

(c) **Withdrawal :** As part of scorched earth policy.

The strategic employment of BW could be as under:-

(a) It could disorganise industry by direct action and morale effect.

(b) Use against plants, crops or animals. In this manner it could have a great effect on a nation's economy.

(c) The aggressor must devise a geographical or time limit so that multiplication of the agent does not affect his own effort and prevent his eventual occupation and use of the strategic area.

Biodefence Measures

Means of Protection

Individual Protection. BW is as yet a little known weapon and it is therefore, difficult to be precise about the best means of defence.[16] Apart from a very high standard of hygiene and cleanliness, which should be the common practice, it would appear that the best means of defence against BW agents released either by bombs or shells or as airborne clouds are the respirator, protective over-garments, and preventive inoculation. These are discussed below:-

(a) **The Respirator and Protective Over-garments :** A well fitted respirator adjusted in time will give complete protection. The problem is to know in time when to put it on. In this respect early warning by intelligence services of the likely use by the enemy of BW agents will be all important. Once CW/BW has begun

16. Christopher F. Chyba, Towards Biological Security, *Foreign Affairs*, May/June 2002, Vol. 81, No.3,p.p.122-136; also n. 15.

respirators and protective over-garments will have to be put on whenever hostile bombing or shelling starts and may have to be worn for long periods.

(b) **Preventive inoculation :** Provided a suitable vaccine is available, preventive inoculation would give a good measure of protection against a biological agent.

There are however, many problems still to be solved and some of these are listed below:-

(a) Even if the required vaccine is available, though at present very few are available against likely BW agents, there is a natural delay in the human body in developing resistance to the disease.

(b) The detection and identification of BW agents is a long and difficult process which may take several weeks. It is difficult to find out what agent the enemy is using and therefore, what disease to inoculate against.

(c) Mass inoculation in the Services is relatively simple, when compared to mass inoculation in the civil population, which would be a gigantic task even if the vaccines were available.

Collective Protection

(a) Shelters. Underground dug-outs fitted with air shelters would prevent contamination of the atmosphere. The normal precautions will reduce the hazard considerably.

(b) **Hygiene and sanitation :** This subject assumes great importance. A very high standard of hygiene and sanitation would be required. Full use should be made of the nation's medical services. Great attention must be paid to: handling, storing and preparation of food; water supply; disposal of refuse; destruction of vermin, flies and pests; and personal hygiene.

Detection

Detection of BW agents is extremely difficult as they cannot be seen, smelt or tasted. Also, they do not react easily to detectors. Even after it is known that BW agents have been used, it will take time to identify the micro-organisms. Some of the available means of detection are: intelligence services, reports on unusual bomb bursts, investigation of sudden outbreaks of disease and so on. The US Army has developed at least two types of equipment for bio-detection and warning; these were tried during the Gulf War. The equipment can also be mounted on a specially designed reconnaissance vehicle.[17]

While nerve agents are easier to produce and weaponise and could act percutaneously against unprotected people, toxins would be more difficult for an enemy to detect, some would be effective in much smaller quantities (submicrogram lethality). Even with conservative assumptions of low toxicity and extremely poor distribution efficiency, a few kilograms of toxin can contaminate a large battlefield. For instance, approximately 15 tons of nerve agent would be required to cause 50 per cent deaths in the exposed population in an area 60 sq. kms. Similar damage would be caused in the same area by one and a half kilogram of botulinum toxin.[18]

Decontamination

After an attack thorough decontamination of ground clothing and personnel will be necessary. Persons exposed to the attack should wash themselves, preferably under a shower. Clothing should be boiled with soap and hung outside to dry. Ground and inside of houses when contaminated should be flushed out with a hose. Any readily available disinfectant can be used. For the above purposes, the US Army has designed a decontaminatine apparatus.

Defence Against Toxin Weapons

A toxin is a toxic substance that can be produced by an animal, plant, or microbe. Some toxins can be produced by molecular biological techniques (protein toxins) or by chemical synthesis (low molecular weight toxins). The most likely route of attack for soldiers or victims of mass terrorism is through the lungs as a result of inhaling a respirable aerosol. The lack of an effect through the skin considerably complicates the attackers' problem. Further, once a toxin has settled out from the air, it is unlikely to

---

17. Albert J. Mauroni, *Chemical-Biological Defence: US Military Policies and Decisions in the Gulf War* (London: Praeger,1998), p.p. 71-90.
18. Malcolm Dando, n.2, p.107.

be sufficiently disturbed again (say, by troop movements) to once again become a respirable aerosol. The threat would, of course, remain from contamination of food or water, until the toxin has degraded.

When considering the toxin threat, what is important is the lethality that can be achieved in a respirable aerosol. The toxin has to be reproducible, storable and stable in an aerosol and possess adequate lethality. Without going into calculations, it would suffice to state that botulinum toxin (a deadly substance) has the level of lethality required for effective use in small quantities. But for toxins less lethal than botulinum toxin or the staphylococcal enterotoxins (for incapacitation), hundreds of kilograms or even tons would be needed to cover an area of 100 sq. kms. with an effective aerosol.

So, for practical reasons, many toxins can be ignored as potential threats. What is important is to recognise the highly lethal toxins , and perhaps the moderately lethal toxins (like ricin), which are easily produced in large quantities. Though many hundreds of the known toxins might be used for assassination, and many tens might be toxic enough to be used as an aerosol in a confined space, only the most highly toxic are of major concern to military forces in regard to large scale open air attack. For example, an armoured or infantry division is not at any great risk of exposure to a marine toxin whose toxicity is so low that 80 tons is needed to produce a Mass Casualty Bio/Toxin Weapon covering an area that a military base may occupy, that is, about 10 sq. kms. Most marine toxins are too difficult to produce in such quantities. Hence, military leaders should be concerned first about the most toxic bacterial toxins—e.g. botulinum toxin, tetanus toxin, diptheria toxin and some others.

Defence Against Bio-regulators

There are difficulties in dispersing peptide bio-regulators. Botulinum toxin, a protein is known to lose its activity quite rapidly when dispersed in the field. But there may well be ways of protecting small peptide agents from environmental degradation or of using non-peptide mimics in place of vulnerable peptides. In future there are likely to be improvements in production capabilities and highly specific analogues of naturally occurring bio-regulators will become available: these are likely to be more potent than the original natural regulator. The substances that might be engineered into a bacterium could damage the nervous system, alter moods, trigger psychological changes, and even kill.

To combat this phenomena the US Defence Advanced Projects Agency has initiated defensive research projects to combat the possible use of biological weapons. The aim of such work essentially is to acquire the ability to detect different types of pathogens extremely rapidly and thus the ability to take effective action against an attack. A US Airforce study concluded that by the year 2020:

The critical aspects of war fighting in CW/BW environment will be solved. Agent detection both on—site and stand- off will be available. In the event of an attack, equipment and critical terrain can be rapidly decontaminated.......Our ability to model this environment, coupled with our known ability to fight successfully under these conditions, will be a major deterrent to the use of CW/BW weapons.[19]

But it is also possible that an arms race of considerable proportions would result as offensive research is attempted order to overcome the strengthened defence.

Conclusion

The outlook for biological weapons is interesting. Weapons research has only just begun to explore the potential of the biotechnological revolution. Many more developments lie ahead than behind. Biotechnology will profoundly change the nature and range of bio-weaponry and the context in which it will be used. Apart from the ability to use pathogens effectively in warfare to harm life, it will be possible to manipulate the processes of cognition, development, reproduction, and inheritance. Should such capabilities be widely used, the nature of human conflict may radically change. New means of violence, coercion and subjugation would become available against which counter-measures have yet to be thought of. Hence, the need to effectively control the offensive and defensive means of BW.

---

19. Scientific Advisory Board, *New World Vistas: Air and Space Power for the 21st Century* (Human Systems/Biotechnology Volume), (US Airforce, Washington DC 1997).

Bioterrorism and the Future

P.R. Chari

The Backdrop

Biological warfare involves the deliberate spreading of disease in humans, animals and plants by introducing living micro-organisms into the victims, that multiply within their hosts, leading to symptoms manifesting themselves after an incubation period. Micro-organisms can also produce toxins—poisonous chemicals—that cause disease. Biological weapons (BWs) are classified as weapons of mass destruction (WMD) along with nuclear and chemical weapons[1], since they can cause mass deaths among humans and livestock and extensive damage to food crops. BWs evoke primordial fears as revealed by the alarm caused in the United States following the anthrax mail attacks in late 2001. Biological warfare is facilitated by three enabling factors.

- First, the diffusion of technology, including biotechnology and genetic engineering, assisted by the global revolution in information technology.
- Second, the mobility of goods and services occasioned by the global revolution in communications also makes easier the spreading of infection.
- Third, indiscriminate use of antibiotics has led to resistance being developed to these drugs, which is hampering the treatment of tuberculosis, malaria and hepatitis—the three greatest killer diseases.

A case for acquiring nuclear weapons rather than BWs can be made since:" The awesome destructive power of the atomic bomb is associated with three fundamental features: visibility, predictability, and immediacy. No other non-conventional weapon can produce as visible, predictable, and rapid destructive effects as NWs."[2] A contrary view holds that,"...if

---

1. They have also been classified as NBC (nuclear-biological-chemical) weapons, and as CBRN (chemical, biological, radiological and nuclear) weapons.
2. Avner Cohen, " Israel and Chemical/ Biological Weapons: History, Deterrence, and Arms Control", *The Nonproliferation Review,* Fall-Winter 2001, Volume 8, Number 3, p. 40.

I were asked, among those nuclear, chemical and biological [weapons], which did I think was the more likely [to be used] and the more worrisome to me at the moment, I probably would say biological. It can be done in relatively small places with dual-use equipment, and there are a variety of delivery mechanisms".[3] Additionally, BWs are cheap, and can be extracted from either their natural source or grown from seed stock obtainable from culture collections available for medical and biological research purposes and rapidly multiplied.

Biological and chemical weapons are popularly believed to be the "poor man's atomic bombs". Two canards regarding BWs, however, need to be urgently dispelled.

- First, great suspicion attaches to the likely transfer of biological weapons to WMD aspirants or non-state actors by "second rung" countries of proliferation concern like China, Egypt, Israel, Iran, Iraq, Libya, North Korea, Syria and Taiwan.[4] There is, however, some irony in this accusatory exercise. The industrialised countries had developed BWs before and during the Second World War, including the United States, former Soviet Union, United Kingdom, Japan, Canada, France and Germany.[5] There is incontrovertible evidence, moreover, of the Japanese Imperial Army's germ-warfare programme during the Second World War. Its infamous Unit 731 used prisoners of war for live experiments with pathogens. The United States currently maintains an active 'biodefence' programme where genetic engineering techniques are being studied. What is being underscored here is that BWs have been actually manufactured, stored, and used by First World countries, whilst suspecting Third World nations of these activities. In truth, the situation obtaining in the former Republics of the Soviet Union should be of greater concern, since, " All the ingredients for successful

---

3. Backgrounder, " Rumsfeld says Possible Biological Attack is Chief Concern", 3 April 2002, p. 2, http:*//usembassy.state.gov/delhi.html*
4. Graham S. Pearson, " The Threat of Deliberate Disease in the 21st Century", in Marie I. Chevrier, Graham S. Pearson, Amy E. Smithson, Jonathan B. Tucker, Gillian R. Woollett, *Biological Weapons Proliferation: Reasons for Concern, Courses of Action,* Report No. 24, January 1998, p. 26.
5. Judith Miller, Stephen Engelberger, William Broad, *Germs: The Ultimate Weapon* (New York: Simon & Schuster, 2001), p. 38.

black marketeering are present throughout the chemical and biological weapons complexes—under-or unemployed scientists and managers, valuable commodities at far-flung locations, and poor security".[6] This situation predicates pathogens being either stolen or lost.

- Second, BWs are often aggregated with Chemical Weapons (CWs) and generically termed chembio weapons. But CWs differ very considerably from BWs. For instance, the location of a CW attack could be discovered, but the site where BWs are released would be very difficult to pinpoint. Chemical weapons take effect almost instantaneously, whereas biological weapons might take days and weeks to manifest themselves. An attack by chemical weapons requires the affected area to be decontaminated, but a BW attack requires the victims to be isolated, quarantined and hospitalised.[7] There is no doubt, however, that all countries, developed and developing, are unprepared and ill equipped to meet the BW threat.

It would be argued in this paper that the challenge to international security from bioterrorism cannot be met without international cooperation. This requires the United States to shed its unilateralist posture and help devise a verification regime for the Biological Weapons Convention that embodies the international norm for tackling the proliferation threat from BWs. Before reaching these conclusions the place of biological weapons in the pantheon of WMDs and biowarfare would be discussed. Further, the contours of bioterrorism, past and future, would be discussed, before suggesting remedial measures for meeting this threat.

Biowarfare in the WMD Pantheon

The quality of delayed action distinguishing biological weapons imbues them with both advantages and disadvantages for use as WMDs. The advantages are that victims would be unaware of being attacked before

---

6. Amy E. Smithson, *Toxic Archipelago: Preventing Proliferation from the Former Soviet Chemical and Biological Weapons Complexes,* The Henry L. Stimson Centre, Report No. 32, December 1999, p. 19.
7. A detailed comparison of the important differences between chemical and biological terrorism may be seen in Donald A. Henderson, " The Looming Threat of Bioterrorism", *Science,* Vol. 283, 26 February 1999, p. 1780 Table 1.

the disease symptoms manifest themselves. Delayed action would permit the perpetrators to distance themselves from the scene of attack, which makes deniability easy, but attribution difficult. These qualities make them attractive for acquisition by weak countries in asymmetrically placed situations because, "biological weapons offer the aggressor potential for deniability, especially if the agent used occurs naturally in the state attacked. All of these factors increase the prospects that the risk of biological warfare may be greater today than in the past". [8] Their greatest disadvantage is that they cannot be utilised for tactical or battlefield purposes. BWs are of little worth also against troops or populations inoculated against such attacks. For instance, the United States is protecting its troops routinely against anthrax by regular inoculation.

Despite these disadvantages, biological weapons are attractive for aspiring proliferators since their manufacture is easily concealable within a legitimate pharmaceutical or biotechnology programme. Highly intrusive verifications are required to discover such activities, but this would not be politically feasible. BWs also possess great versatility—they can be used selectively against human beings, livestock or food crops. Indeed, the likelihood of livestock and agriculture being targeted by terrorist organisations using BWs is gaining greater recognition now. An extreme view urges that BW terrorism against human beings is a 'high-consequence, low-probability event', but a biological attack that targets agriculture 'should be regarded as a high-consequence, high probability' event and receive the attention it deserves as a grave national security risk". [9] Their cheapness, ease of manufacture and concealment, could make BWs the weapons of choice for aberrant states and non-state actors.

Proceeding further, anti-human biological agents suited for biowarfare include bacteria causing anthrax, bubonic plague, brucellosis and tularemia; rickettsiae causing Q-fever; virus causing Venezuelan equine encephalitis; and toxins like saxitoxin, botulinum, ricin and

---

8. Graham S. Pearson, " The Threat of Deliberate Disease in the 21st Century", p. 36.
9. See, for instance, Rocco Casagrande, " Biological Terrorism Targeted at Agriculture: The Threat to US National Security", *The Nonproliferation Review,* Fall-Winter 2000, Volume 7, Number 3, p. 93.

Staphylococcus enterotoxin that lead to a variety of symptoms and even death.[10] The most useful biowarfare agents have been narrowed down to four: smallpox, plague, anthrax and botulism, but the US bioweapons programme revealed virtually insurmountable problems in producing and dispensing militarily relevant quantities of plague organisms and botulism toxins. By a process of elimination, therefore, anthrax and smallpox become the weapons of choice for biowarfare because," Smallpox and anthrax have other advantages in that they can be grown reasonably easily and in large quantities and are sturdy organisms that are resistant to destruction. They are thus suitable for aerosol dissemination to reach large areas and numbers of people".[11] Greater anxiety should attach to emerging trends and advances in biotechnology, which could be used to synthesise biowarfare agents. These new technologies include, "combinatorial chemistry, genomics, microarrays, proteomics, toxicogenomics, and database mining",[12] which have relevance to finding new drugs, but also to developing new biological weapons.

The value of a biological agent or toxin for biowarfare, incidentally, increases with its capacity for aerosolisation, which can cause high casualties and secondary infections, but also the unavailability of vaccines for prophylaxis. Nevertheless, two major problems persist with using biological agents and toxins as weapons.

- First, their production in militarily significant quantities, more true of toxins, is difficult. Thus, " eight tons of contaminated Alaskan butter clams were needed to make one gram of saxitoxin, and it proved impossible to extract militarily significant quantities of red-tide toxin".[13]
- The second problem concerns their dissemination. Being living organisms they cannot be used in munitions, as they would be

---

10. Graham S. Pearson, " The Threat of Deliberate Disease in the 21st Century", Table I, pp. 18-19, describes the rate of action, effective dosage and symptoms/ effects.
11. Donald A. Henderson, " The Looming Threat of Bioterrorism", p. 1281.
12. Mark Wheelis, " Biotechnology and Biochemical Weapons", *The Nonproliferation Review,* Spring 2002, Vol. 9, No. 1, p. 49.
13. Kathleen C. Bailey, *Doomsday Weapons in the Hands of Many: The Arms Control Challenge of the '90s* (Urbana and Chicago: University of Illinois Press, 1991), p. 93.

destroyed by heat and shock; hence the most effective means of delivery is dispersion by a spraying mechanism. "A delivery system must therefore have two attributes. First, the delivery system needs to expel the agent efficiently from its container. Second, assuming an agent that attacks through the respiratory system, the delivery system must produce 1 to 10 micron sized particles of agent".[14]

These difficulties are by no means insurmountable. Commercially available equipment like agricultural sprayers or light aircraft can disseminate biological agents using prevailing winds to target the intended victims. It is also possible for BWs to be delivered by other means like water supply sources, mass transit systems and vents in buildings.

Bioterrorism as the Means of Biowarfare

Biological weapons and terrorism are not new problems. Violence by biological means has an ancient lineage, and includes poisoning wells by throwing corpses into them or catapulting dead bodies infected with smallpox into besieged cities or supplying blankets infected with smallpox to American Indians.[15] The use of violence to prevail on societies to make radical social or political changes at the behest of committed individuals or groups is as old as history itself. 9/11, however, anointed transnational terrorism as being the most serious threat to international security. It highlighted the nexus between terrorist states (Afghanistan), terrorist organisations (Taliban and Al Qaeda) and their unhesitating willingness to cause mass destruction. The utilisation of innovative means like airliners as WMDs highlights the likelihood of terrorists using exotic armaments, which could include biological agents and toxins.

The use of WMDs by non-state actors has long been debated as a theoretical possibility, despite evidence accumulating that terrorists could resort to bioterrorism to achieve their ends. Bioterrorism is an aspect of asymmetric warfare, which equalises the weak and the strong, and enables a weak nation to respond militarily against a strong nation seeking full spectrum dominance. An aspect of bioterrorism that is not sufficiently recognised is the mass psycogenic ailments possible by a BW terrorist

14. *Op. cit.*, p; 23.
15. These examples are cited in Wendy Barnaby, *The Plague Makers*, p. 6.

attack. Even unfounded rumours of such an attack can lead to extreme anxieties bordering on psychological illness.

Some early examples of non-state actors showing interest in biological weapons includes information that members of the Weather Underground were planning to steal germs from the Bacteriological Warfare centre at Fort Detrick, Maryland in 1970; organisers of Rise, a group dedicated to creating a new master race, being arrested in 1972 for plotting to poison Chicago's water system with typhoid bacteria; and technical military manuals on germ warfare being found in a San Francisco hideout of the Symbionese Liberation Army.[16] In a celebrated case members of the Rajneesh cult contaminated salad bars in Oregon with *Salmonella typhi* in September 1984, which causes typhoid fever, to secure a particular outcome in a local election. Nobody was killed but around 750 persons became ill. [17] An exhaustive study of bioterrorism " has chronicled 52 confirmed cases [in] this [20th] century in which terrorists, criminals or others expressed interest in biological agents...which resulted in 982 victims, including nine deaths, [and] were intended to achieve various ends: murder, extortion, incapacitation, mass murder, terror, making a political statement, and revenge". [18]

A study conducted by the US Senate in May 1996 concluded, "The threat of a terrorist group using a nuclear, biological or chemical weapon of mass destruction in the United States is real. It is not a matter of 'if' but rather 'when' such an event will occur".[19] These perceptions gained salience after the 9/11 attacks, leading to beliefs that terrorists have demonstrated " suicidal tendencies and are beyond deterrence...we must

---

16. Yonah Alexander," Terrorism and High-Technology Weapons", in Lawrence Zelic Freedman and Yonah Alexander, *Perspectives on Terrorism* (Delhi: Hindustan Publishing Corporation (India), 1985), Indian Reprint, p. 230.
17. Judith Miller, Stephen Engelberg, William Broad, *Germs:* pp. 15-33 documents this case.
18. Wendy Barnaby, *The Plague Makers,* p. 36. Seth Carus of the National Defence University in Washington has enumerated these cases, but excluded State-sponsored acts of terrorism like the Bulgarian Secret Police assassinating the political leader, Georgi Markov, using ricin.
19. *Op. cit.,* p., 35-6 citing Staff Statement, US Senate Permanent Subcommittee on Investigations (Minority Staff), Hearings on Global Proliferation of Weapons of Mass Destruction: Response to Domestic Terrorism, 27 March 1996.

anticipate that they will use weapons of mass destruction if allowed the opportunity. The minimum standard for victory in this war (against terrorism) is the prevention of any of the individual terrorists or terrorist cells from obtaining"[20] these weapons. Three contemporary events have drawn further attention to bioterrorism. They are:

- First, the 1995 sarin (a nerve gas) attack by the Aum Shinrikyo sect in the Tokyo subway, which killed 12 but led to some 5500 persons being injured. Subsequent investigations revealed this sect's efforts to produce and disseminate botulinus toxin by spraying it around Tokyo from a moving vehicle, and from a multistoreyed building. That these attacks did not succeed is fortuitous. The motives of the Aum were as bizarre as their actions; apparently they believed an apocalyptic war was imminent that would permit them to gain control of Japan and the world.[21] These attacks are significant because they demolished an important psychological barrier prohibiting the use of CBWs against civilian populations. Indeed, they confirmed that some terrorists were "beyond deterrence".

- Second, a large number of anthrax mail attacks—both real and imagined—came to light in the United States after 9/11. They involved anthrax spores in granulated form being randomly dispatched to five people " using plain envelopes and 34-cent stamps. Twenty-three people contracted anthrax, and 5 people lost their lives".[22] These attacks caused great alarm, and " made the American public more fearful than it had been at any time since the Cuban Missile Crisis".[23] The psychological insecurity caused in the United States by dispatch of anthrax

---

20. Statement made by Senator Richard Lugar (Republican, Indiana). " US Goal: Keep Weapons of Mass Destruction out of Terrorist's Hands", The Washington File, dated 13 March 2002, US Department of State, *http://usinfo.state.gov.*
21. Donald A. Henderson, " The Looming Threat of Bioterrorism", *Science,* p. 1280; " Bolton Cites need to Respond to Biological Weapons Threat", Official Text dated 28 August 2002, p. 3, *http://usembassy.state.gov/delhi.html;* and Wendy Barnaby, *The Plague Makers,* pp. 31-33.
22. Official Text, " Bolton Cites Need to Respond to Biological Weapons Threat". 28 August 2002, p. 3, *http://www. Usembassy.State.gov/delhi.html*
23. Peter J. Roman, " The Dark Winter of Biological Terrorism", *Orbis,* Summer 2002, p. 469.

mail to American politicians and media persons reinforces beliefs that non-state actors could use BWs to cause both casualties and socio-economic disruption. An unexpected lesson from this episode is that developing bio-defence capabilities can facilitate bioterrorism. Evidence is growing that the type of anthrax used, "Ames Strain", came from US army stocks held in Fort Detrick. Suspicions have focused on a former employee perpetrating these attacks, since the skills required to culture, prepare and deliver weapons-grade anthrax spores are only available to a handful of scientists working in this area; hence the suspect list has been narrowed down to a very few individuals.[24] The problem is that the kind of proof that would stand up in court is not yet available.

Three important findings can be reached from these anthrax mail attacks:

- First, the difficulty in investigating them is Herculean if the suspects belong to the biodefence community, where the investigators would encounter secrecy restrictions and *espirit d'corps* problems in proceeding with their enquiries.
- Second, the knee-jerk conclusion in the US that some terrorist group in the Third World was responsible for these attacks is not true; ample evidence points to disgruntled or motivated individuals in the United States—however incomprehensible their motivations—being responsible. An obvious case is that of the Oklahoma bomber.
- Third, considerable evidence has accumulated that Osama bin Laden had an interest in manufacturing WMDs, including biological weapons. A CIA report

24. Guy Gugliotta, " Still No Arrests in Anthrax Probe, but ' Progress' is Noted", *Washington Post,* 4 August 2002; " The Hunt for the Anthrax Killer", *Newsweek,* 12 August 2002; and Laura Rozen, " Who is Steven Hatfill? The FBI has searched a US bio-warfare scientist's apartment as part of its anthrax investigation", *The American Prospect Online,* 12 June 2002 at *http://www. Prospect-Org/webfeatures/2002/06/rozen-1-06-27.html*

informs that bin Laden has sought CBRN materials to further his goals. "Since the early 1990s, bin Laden has pursued the development of chemical and biological weapons and revealed a longstanding interest in nuclear materials. A senior bin Laden associate on trial in Egypt claimed in 1999 that his group had chemical and biological weapons...terrorist groups are most interested in chemicals. ...We see lesser interest in biological materials that appears focused on agents for use in small-scale poisonings or assassinations".[25]

This long citation informs that no government can discount the growing evidence of Osama bin Laden and terrorist organisations using BWs to progress their political or religious objectives. Osama bin Laden " has professed the acquisition of " weapons of mass destruction" (WMD) to be a "religious duty". Reports that documents retrieved from Al-Qaida facilities in Afghanistan contain information on CRBN materials underscore bin Laden's rhetoric".[26] His vision of a restored Caliphate envisages the State enjoying both temporal and religious power; anyone opposing this vision is an apostate whose destruction becomes a pious duty. This doctrine of religious totalitarianism is really a form of fascism. Such individuals and groups cannot be deterred, but their threats of apocalyptic vengeance and annihilation cannot be ignored.

Two other events in the recent past have reinforced the threat of bioterrorism. They are the discovery of a vast and sophisticated biological weapons programme in the former Soviet Union that could fall into the hands of aberrant states and terrorist organisations, and the discovery of a significant BW programme in Iraq, which is currently providing the rationale for the contemplated US attack on Iraq to displace Saddam Hussein. BWs from these stocks becoming available to terrorists is no longer a theoretical proposition.

A short digression is necessary to analyse the psychology of a new

---

25. Official Text, " New CIA Report Documents Global Weapons Proliferation Trends", 1 February 2002, *http://usembassy. State.gov/ delhi.html*, p. 11.
26. *Patterns of Global Terrorism 2001,* (United States Department of State: Washington, May 2002), p. 66.

breed of terrorists afflicting the world. It is arguable that terrorists with a rational cause would wish to avoid inflicting mass casualties since they want "a lot of people *watching,* not a lot of people *dead";*[27] hence they would not transgress certain ethical boundaries and indulge in senseless violence to damage their cause. Further, the handling of BWs is a hazardous enterprise, not without risks to its users. These rational considerations may not sway the new genre of religious terrorists that believes in "the idea that sacrificing oneself to a " higher calling" through violence is a way for recruits to fulfil spiritual, emotional and in some cases financial needs. They offer posthumous fame after suicide bombing campaigns and the hope of rewards in the afterlife". [28] Religious cults attract followers inspired by mystical and divinely inspired motives or driven by blind hatred of racial or ethnic groups, which places them beyond the pale of rational discourse. Suicide terrorism is an aspect of this phenomenon, which the 9/11 airline hijackers dramatically highlighted. This new genre of religious terrorists has attracted humiliated young persons, inured to an atmosphere of violence, and without the desire to live any longer. In their view, " the true faith is supposedly in jeopardy, emergency conditions prevail. The killing of innocents becomes... religiously and morally permissible". [29]

Proceeding further, the psychiatric reasons motivating terrorists have been encapsulated within four hypotheses in order of psychic depth but decreasing plausibility. They are the re-affirmation of self-esteem; depersonalisation or the abandoning of individuality to serve the interests of a larger group; the establishment of intimacy with the victim by enforcing his recognition; and a belief in the magic of violence to dedicate human powers in the service of superhuman or godlike figures. [30] In conclusion, "A person who joins a group that takes over the responsibility

---

27. Brian M. Jenkins, " Understanding the Link between Motives and Methods", in Brad Roberts, (ed.) *Terrorism with Chemical and Biological Weapons: Calibrating Risks and Responses* (Arlington, Va: The Chemical and Biological Arms Institute, 1997), p. 45
28. Jessica Stern, " Get to the roots of terrorism", *International Herald Tribune,* 26 April 2002.
29. *Ibid.*
30. Lawrence Zelic Freedman, "Terrorism: Problems of the Polistaraxic", in Lawrence Zelic Freedman and Yonah Alexander, *Perspectives on Terrorism,* pp. 3-5.

for his actions does not exist any more; therefore, the group can send him to perform suicidal missions. The group is responsible only for his destruction, not for his existence; by joining it, he has already ceased to exist as an individual...Terrorism is just the last stage in the age of revolutions, the last step in a trend towards social and cultural disintegration. The direction is towards self-negation". [31] These perspectives would make it apparent that terrorists seeking to use BWs have deep resentments that need addressing; quick-fix solutions are unlikely to provide the right answers to handling a complex problem.

The foregoing permits an estimation of the likelihood of bioterrorism constituting a future threat, especially in the light of the anthrax mail attacks in the United States. The CIA report cited above warns against terrorists using chemical, biological, radiological and nuclear (CBRN) materials, whilst assessing that they would continue to rely on bombings and shootings.[32] . Terrorist groups contemplating BW use would find it easier to acquire them from existing stocks in the former Soviet Union or other biodefence programmes rather than to manufacture biological weapons by their own efforts. Terrorists could, however, be satisfied with developing biological weapons of lower efficiency and lethality to inflict fewer casualties but create alarm and cause disruption in the community for drawing attention to their political agenda. The scepticism about terrorists using BWs is founded on the reasonable belief that their production to military standards requires sophisticated facilities with high safety standards to ensure that they would not infect themselves. This is valid, but BWs have been produced in primitive conditions. For instance, "During the Second World War, the UK produced cattle cakes containing anthrax and the people doing this put anthrax spores into the centre of the cakes without wearing respirators. They worked in a little shed behind a sheet of glass".[33]

The likelihood of these eventualities can be rated low on rational calculations. But the damage to life portended by a BW attack suggests that national security establishments must plan for the worst whilst hoping

31. *Op. cit.,* p. 17.
32. Official Text, " New CIA Report Documents Global Weapons Proliferation Trends", p. 11.
33. Wendy Barnaby, *The Plague Makers,* pp. 40-1. citing personal interview with Graham Pearson.

for the best. On prudential grounds therefore no government can ignore the dangers of bioterrorism. This might explain a significant development regarding smallpox virus. With the worldwide eradication of smallpox only two depositories of its vaccine remain, located in the United States and Russia. They were to be destroyed several years ago, but this decision was deferred from time to time. Now, the 191 members of the World Health Organisation have reversed their earlier decision to destroy these stocks, and decided to retain them for research into new vaccines and treatment.[34] Israel and Britain are acquiring stocks of smallpox vaccine, whilst the United States and Russia are considering proposals to start vaccinating their population against the disease. These decisions are informed by fears of bioterrorism. [35] More precisely, the fear obtains that, " A mixture of rogue states and well-financed religious cults with scientists desperately seeking funds creates a volatile situation with potentially serious consequences".[36]

We can now turn our attention to what prophylactic, preventive and countermeasures can be taken to defend against bioterrorism.

Remedial Measures

Before discussing these measures, the difficulties of grappling with a BW attack must be appreciated. Five problems have been highlighted, including non-availability of adequate vaccine stocks in the area infected and cater for secondary cases; reluctance to view an outbreak of disease as a security threat; difficulty in identifying a disease outbreak as having been deliberately caused, lest it alarm people; difficulty in determining whether second-generation cases are due to contagion or new attacks; and that, if detection is delayed, the victims become unwitting agents to spread the disease.[37] These dilemmas highlight that defending against bioterrorism, an aspect of homeland (internal) security, requires close coordination between the government and civil society organisations.

The new US strategy to counter the threat of BW proliferation is predicated on a full range of tightened export controls, intensified non-proliferation

---

34. William J. Broad and Judith Miller, " Others Follow US On Smallpox Vaccine", *The New York Times,* 25 April 2002.
35. AP news item, " Smallpox Virus", *The Indian Express,* 20 May 2002.
36. Donald A Henderson, " The Looming Threat of Bioterrorism", p. 1281.
37. Peter J. Roman, " The Dark Winter of Biological Terrorism", pp. 476-9.

dialogue, increased domestic preparedness and controls, enhanced biodefence and counterterrorism capabilities, and innovative measures against disease outbreaks, as well as the full compliance by all States Parties with the global ban".[38] It appears, however, that the technology denial modality has gained salience with the rigors of the Australia Group's guidelines increasing to deny materials, equipment and technology to countries of concern. The abandoning of negotiations on a Verification Protocol for the BTWC will further heighten the importance of the Australia Group.

Coming to measures that states could take to protect themselves against bioterrorism ten are of significance:

- First, the imperative need for domestic legislation is underscored to "prohibit and prevent the development, production, stockpiling, acquisition or retention of the agents, toxins, weapons, equipment and means of delivery" of BWs as envisaged in Article IV of the BWTC. Possessing these agents and toxins or aiding prohibited activities should be made a criminal offence. Further steps are required to ensure the physical safety and protection of identified biological agents and toxins and regulate their transfer for legitimate purposes. End use verification procedures would greatly add to the credibility of these measures. The US has recently finalised legislation to expand its stockpiles of antibiotics and vaccines, tighten regulation of laboratories handling dangerous microbes, improve food safety, protect water supply systems and speed up the approval of new medicines.[39]
- Second, export controls need to be imposed for giving effect to the external dimensions of Article III. Developing countries have argued that export controls administered by the Australia Group adversely impinges on the promise in Article X that States Parties would facilitate "the fullest possible exchange of equipment, materials and scientific and technological information for the use of bacteriological (biological) agents and toxins for peaceful

38. Fact Sheet, " The Biological Weapons Convention", US Department of State, Bureau of Arms Control, 22 May 2002, *http://usembassy. State.gov/delhi.html* p. 1,
39. Robert Pear, " Negotiators Reach Compromise on Measures to Strengthen Safeguards against Bioterror", *The New York Times,* 22 May 2002.

purposes". A via media solution is needed to reconcile the regulatory provisions of Article III with the developmental promise in Article X. A technology denial/ control regime for biological agents and toxins would be difficult to implement, shifting the emphasis on national technical means to verify end use compliance. Realistically, however, technology control/ denial regimes are unlikely to deter terrorists or address the problem of sensitive materials leaking from the former Republics of the Soviet Union or stem the emigration of its qualified scientists and engineers to aspirant nations Developed countries must also appreciate that export controls are only one instrument in an overall anti-terrorism strategy that must address several other related issues.

- Third, the problem of losing control over the vast stocks of BWs in Russia needs urgent attention. A new G-8 Global Partnership against the Spread of Weapons and Materials of Mass Destruction has recently been formed to focus on issues of non-proliferation, disarmament, counterterrorism and nuclear safety, starting with Russia. Guidelines for new and expanded cooperation in the non-proliferation sphere have been established. A " debt option" has been created by which the US "would agree in advance to waive collection of a given amount of debt payments... Russia would [then] be able to make expanded budgetary expenditures for agreed non-proliferation activities". [40] The G-8 countries might extend this modality to other countries known to be manufacturing and stocking BWs.

- Fourth, a large stockpile of vaccines and antibiotics needs being created in storage centers around the world for utilisation by countries that suffer an attack. This stockpiling is necessary because it is obviously impossible to manufacture large quantities of antibiotics and vaccines in a short period of time. No one country, moreover, could bear the costs of carrying these large stockpiles that have a discrete shelf life, after which they must be discarded. The US is taking steps to increase its national stockpile of antibiotics and vaccines.

---

40. Official Text, " Larson Praises G-8 Initiative to Combat WMD Proliferation", 26 July 2002, *http://usembassy. state.gov/delhi.html,* pp. 2-3.

- Fifth, the strengthening of intelligence capabilities to detect and prevent terrorist activities is of the essence. This is a complex issue, since bioterrorism is an aspect of WMD terrorism, which is an adjunct of international terrorism. The eradication of international terrorism requires the linked phenomenon of money laundering, arms/ drugs smuggling, crime syndicates and so on being addressed. The urgent need, therefore, obtains for meaningful international cooperation, especially in the areas of intelligence sharing, border control, watching over suspicious financial flows and undertaking joint operations against terrorist groups.

- Sixth, international cooperation must embrace a multiple nation effort to undertake a global research programme for developing new and cheaper drug regimes for use against biowarfare diseases. For instance, feasibility studies show that production of improved second-generation vaccines can be quickly developed.[41] There were, incidentally, some doubts about the anthrax vaccine being used to protect US troops; [42] so further investigations were necessitated to ascertain their efficacy and safety. A larger research effort is also required to develop plant types that are resistant to pest attacks that might be deliberately contrived. There is, further, the problem of treating genetically modified biological agents and toxins that might not yield to known vaccines and lines of treatment. This would also be true of disease vectors released in aerosolised form, since the vaccines presently available are generally designed for use against the ingested form of the disease. The first indication of a BW attack would be the onset of an epidemic; so no prior warning would be available to take prophylactic or preventive measures to protect against the disease. Hence, these research questions need being urgently addressed.

- Seventh, the prophylactic and preventive measures devised may have to be different for the armed forces and the civilian population. The former would need to be provided a range of

---

41. Donald A. Henderson, "The Looming Threat of Bioterrorism", p. 1282.
42. For details of this controversy, see Wendy Barnaby, *The Plague Makers,* p. 149.

protective measures in anticipation of being deliberately targeted in a limited theatre; whether this is necessary or feasible for widely dispersed civilian populations requires urgent consideration by the medical fraternity and civil defence officials.

- Eighth, a difficult decision to be pondered over is whether a health education programme should be initiated for the civilian population, lest awareness of a bioterrorist attack cause alarm and encourage psychosomatic symptoms.[43] The need to educate physicians and nurses about bioterrorism, the diseases that could be spread, their recognition, and lines of treatment is, however, essential.
- Ninth, the need for devising a plan to provide passive defence measures for protecting the population, including the means to detect a bioterrorist attack, planning medical counter-measures and contamination control requires a public health approach being adopted. Greater networking between public health authorities and hospitals in the private sector is imperative, as also between laboratories spread across the country and the world. There is no experience of such collaborative working in the past.
- Tenth, social science research must study the linkages between non-state actors and their bias towards WMDs, including bioweapons. Religious terrorism, including suicide terrorism, also demands greater attention to discern the roots of such abnormal behaviour for devising countermeasures.

Conclusions

Bioterrorism, an aspect of international terrorism, like other forms of transnational crime, cannot be tackled by unilateral action; hence nations must cooperate with each other to deal with this menace. This is especially true if the root causes of terrorism are to be addressed, which largely derives from the sense of injustice in the oppressed and deprived, leading

---

43. An unlearnt lesson of the Bhopal Gas Tragedy is that people living in the vicinity of the Union Carbide plant were unaware of the symptoms and remedies to deal with any leakage of methyl isocyanate that caused the deaths. Since this chemical is water-soluble, covering their faces with a wet cloth could have saved the affected population, had this been known to them earlier.

to anger, hatred and the irrational violence. Regrettably, the United States has anointed unilateralism as its *leitmotif* to pursue its perceived national self-interests, whilst demanding international cooperation in its war against terrorism. The milieu, therefore, for securing this international cooperation is just not there.

The US role in withdrawing from the eight-year-old global negotiations on a Verification Protocol, designed to provide teeth to the Biological Weapons Convention, after six years of negotiations has been unique. There are certainly problems in detecting clandestine BW activities within a legitimate research or pharmaceutical or biotech programme due to its ease of concealment and destruction of proof, dual-purpose nature of such action and so on. But the drastic US step of withdrawing altogether from these negotiations has eviscerated them of all meaning. Officially it was stated that, " The United States rejected the draft protocol for three reasons: first, it was based on a traditional arms control approach that will not work on biological weapons; second, it would have compromised national security and confidential business information; and third, it would have been used by proliferators to undermine other effective international export control regimes". [44]

By way of alternate steps to combat the threat from biological weapons the United States proposes to rely on a mix of national and multilateral measures. They include the Patriot Act (October 2001) to equip officials with the resources to counter terrorist activities; the Public Health Security and Bioterrorist Preparedness and Response Act (June 2002) to strengthen bio-defence activities; a commitment of funds by the G-8 countries (June 2002) to finance projects to reduce proliferation risks emanating from the former Soviet Union; strengthening health surveillance by WHO members (May 2002) to detect BW attacks and international response; improving NATO's ability to combat BW attacks by stockpiling medicines and protective equipment (May 2002); and tougher export measures by the Australia Group to control items that could be used to manufacture BWs (June 2002).[45]
The Review Conference to discuss the workings of the Biological

---

44. Official Text, " Bolton Cites Need to Respond to Biological Weapons Treaty", 28 August 2002, p. 3, *http://usembassy. State.gov/delhi.html*
45. *Op. cit.*, pp. 5-6.

Weapons Convention had met last year, but was adjourned on 7 December 2001. It was reconvened on 11 November 2002. In line with the prognosis made earlier the Bush administration pressed its beliefs that the revisions to the Verification Protocol favoured by the European Union and other countries will not work, and that it should not be salvaged. The Final Document adopted by the Review Conference three annual meetings taking place in 2003, 2004 and 2005 with the Sixth Review Conference scheduled for 2006. The issues for discussion at these annual conferences include the adoption of national legislation, maintaining security over pathogenic microorganisms and toxins, enhancing capabilities for dealing with alleged BW attack or suspicious outbreaks of disease, strengthening efforts to detect, diagnose and combat infectious diseases, and promulgate a code of conduct for scientists. These laudable measures would address the issue of implementing the BWC and, thereby, the problem of bioterrorism in an oblique fashion. It seems imperative therefore that individual countries sensitise their security establishments, give thought to the dangers of bioterrorism and take precautions before the crisis arises.

The Anthrax Scare

Vivek Shankar Mathur
Arpit Rajain

History records infamy more famously. At forty-six minutes past eight on a September morning, time stood still as a stunned nation and a shocked world watched. The events that unfolded since then have been firmly etched in the collective memory of the American people, and the entire international community. A year has passed, since the heart of America was attacked, when more than anything else, its liberalism was held hostage to a ghastly terrorist attack that took the lives of several innocent civilians going about their daily lives.

Hardly had America recovered from the attacks on the World Trade Centre towers, than a more confusing, and frightening, situation emerged. Allen Ginsberg had once said, "There's nothing to be learnt from history any more, we're in science fiction now."[1] The present world crisis of Biological Weapons as Weapons of Mass Destruction certainly belongs to the latter genre. Once the domain of movies, mad scientists and grisly comic books, the ugly mien of terror just took a turn for the worse. Beginning 18 September, letters containing finely spored, (at over trillion spores per gram) chemically fluffed, aerosolised dry powdered anthrax were being circulated in the US mail. These attacks continued till December 2001. Anthrax tainted letters were first mailed to large media houses like the National Broadcasting Corporation (NBC) and the New York Post. By 4 October, the first reported case of anthrax came from Boca Raton, Florida. Within five days similar letters reached senior government officials, notably Democratic Senators Tom Daschle and Patrick Leahy. Cutaneous anthrax cases were reported by the 12th. There were over two thousand reports of anthrax infections in little over a fortnight since 1 October. Anthrax contaminated mail pouches were also found in US embassies in Peru and Lithuania, exacerbating already heightened feelings of fear, vulnerability and grief. Initially the American media raised accusing fingers

---

1 Quoted in Christopher Butler, "After the Wake: An Essay on the Contemporary Avant-garde", Clarendon Press, (1980)

at Al Qaeda and then Iraq, but later pointed out that the source of these letters was probably domestic. It is generally believed that the anthrax strain that was distributed was no more than two years old.

The Aum Shinrikyo Sarin gas attacks in Tokyo in 1995 [2] set a deadly precedent. Perhaps more than the fatalities, the strong psychological reaction that they evoked heightened the sense of unease. Fears of disease and poison are deep rooted within the human psyche in every culture, playing on our primal fears. The events of September and October 2001 really proved that the threat from biological terrorism is a very real one. If diseases can be used as weapons, the spectrum of counter measures, and threat assessment is prodigious.

What is Anthrax, and is it a WMD?

Anthrax is primarily an affliction of grazing animals. When multiplying in an infected animal, the bacteria, *Bacillus anthracis* are rod-shaped. But anthrax bacteria from the dead or dying animal, upon exposure to oxygen, form a tough-shelled ovoid spore within themselves that can remain dormant and infectious for years. But when an animal swallows or inhales these spores, they come to life, and exude a protein which allows them to burrow into the white blood cells called macrophages, that normally destroy bacteria. But safe inside their host, anthrax bacilli shed their shells, multiply explosively, and swarm out into the bloodstream. There they keep dividing, producing toxins that cause the victim to go into toxic shock and die.

Human anthrax has three major clinical forms: cutaneous, inhalation, and gastrointestinal. Cutaneous anthrax is a result of introduction of the spore through the skin; inhalation anthrax, through the respiratory tract; and gastrointestinal anthrax, by ingestion. *Bacillus anthracis*, the etiologic agent of anthrax, is a large, gram-positive, nonmotile, spore-forming bacterial rod. The three virulence factors of *Bacillns. anthracis* are edema toxin, lethal toxin and a capsular antigen. If untreated, anthrax in all its forms can lead to septicemia and death. Early treatment of cutaneous anthrax is usually curable, and early treatment of all its forms is important for recovery. Patients with gastrointestinal anthrax have reported case- fatality rates ranging from 25 per cent to 75 per cent. Case-

---

3. For more details see http://www.cns.miis.edu.

fatality rates for inhalational anthrax are thought to approach 90 to 100 per cent.

In science, the formula for estimating risk is as follows:[3]

RISK = HAZARD # EXPOSURE

(Risk is the magnitude and likelihood of adverse effect.
Hazard is the harm the agent will cause.
Exposure relates to what population will be exposed to the agent, at what concentration, and for how long.)

For humans, the source of infection in naturally acquired disease is infected livestock and wild animals or contaminated animal products. Human-to-human transmission is extremely unlikely and only reported with cutaneous anthrax. Cutaneous anthrax is the most common manifestation of naturally acquired infection with *Baalks anthracis*. Inhalation (pulmonary) anthrax occurs in persons working in certain occupations where spores may be forced into the air from contaminated animal products, such as animal hair processing.

Anthrax spores are tough, fairly easy to culture and have a long shelf-life. They also survive delivery via bombs, shells or sprays better than many other pathogens. A human with anthrax cannot infect someone else, which could be seen as useful on a battlefield. Spores released in a fine, inhalable mist—the main difficulty with mass administration of anthrax—should affect only the target troops, rather than creating an epidemic which could rebound on the attacker. This might limit the appeal of anthrax—although being unable to diagnose it until it is too late.

The low technology required to produce bio weapons does lend itself to proliferant State and potential terrorist use. These agents can be made fairly easily in dairies, breweries, and most commercial facilities. But there are crucial technical problems that have to be overcome to produce an effective BW. The nature of these problems can be discerned from the case of developing an Anthrax weapon, where the most important part of the process is to create and disperse spores containing particles of exactly

---

3. "Assessing The Threat of Bioterrorism" Congressional Testimony by Raymond Zilinskas, available at http://www.cns.miis.edu, accessed on 17 August 2001.

the right size for inhalation, between 1 and 5 micrometers. The problem is not actually making the culture, but processing it into a form suitable for dispersal, which means drying it, adjusting particle size and loading it into a suitable delivery system. Testing the weapon would be very difficult. Thus weaponising a natural pathogen is quite difficult— this requires systematic effort, practical laboratory skills, and luck! Grinding the powder to particles of the desired diameter is the trickiest part of the process, mostly because of the danger of contamination.

The failure of the Aum Shinrikyo to aerosolise respirable anthrax in 1993 is quite interesting. Even after hiring scientific personnel and investing a great deal in weaponising the pathogen, they failed. Even assuming would-be terrorists had the technical know-how for producing mass quantities of powdered anthrax without infecting producers and contaminating surroundings, it would also require considerable financial investment. Taking delivery systems into account, once released into the air, these spores then become subject to atmospheric conditions. If conditions are gusty, spore dispersal will run into harmless concentrations. Not enough wind, the spores will fall to the ground and not rise again in harmful concentrations. Experts believe that airplanes dusting a city would be an unlikely choice for spreading anthrax spores. The few spores entering buildings would mostly settle; the few that did not would likely be insufficient in concentration to cause infection. Outside, spores would likely fall to the ground or be blown away and rendered effete.

Yet, anthrax, while an unlikely weapon of mass destruction is very easily capable of being very destructive to human life. An accidental release of anthrax spores at a Soviet bioweapons facility, the Centre for Military-Technical Problems of Anti-Bacteriological Defence laboratory in Sverdlovsk (now Yekaterinburg) in 1979 resulted in 70 deaths. In the former Soviet Union, Kirov, Sverdlovsk, and Zagorsk, and the Biopreparat center in Stepnogorsk, worked on anthrax, tularemia, brucellosis, plague, typhus, Q fever, smallpox, botulinum toxin, and Venezuelan equine encephalitis.[4] The experiments were conducted on horses, monkeys, sheep, and donkeys, and on laboratory animals such as white mice, guinea

4. "Former Soviet Biological Weapons Facilities in Kazakhstan: Past, Present, and Future" CNS Occasional Paper available online at http://www.cns.miis.edu, accessed on 17 August 2001.

5. *Ibid.*

pigs, and hamsters.[5] The Scientific Experimental and Production Base (SNOPB) at Stepnogorsk continued research and development work on anthrax that previously had been conducted at the MOD institute in Sverdlovsk, but had to be curtailed in 1979 after an accidental release of anthrax spores from the facility. According to estimates by Western experts, the SNOPB facility, once mobilised, could produce 300 metric tons of weapons-grade anthrax over a ten-month period.[6] In early 1990 Russian President Boris Yeltsin acknowledged that the outbreak was caused by an accidental release of anthrax spores from a Soviet military microbiological facility.[7]

Whatever the limitations of biological weapons, they are still deadly. Perhaps not as weapons of mass destruction, but certainly in limited areas, they can be lethal, even in their crude form. But the problem does not end here. With the growing number of educated persons joining terrorist organisations, and the flood of information from the Internet, that day may not be far away when we are forced to see a more terrible threat, that of developing genetically modified pathogens to produce a new pathogen with increased lethality, greater resistance to antibiotics, and more robust to the environment. Surely this deviance is not unforeseeable. Steps must be taken to tackle this new threat immediately.

Some Essential Elements of the Anthrax Bacteria[8]

- Anthrax bacteria produce spores that can easily become airborne.
- Mail sorting machines can easily aerosolise anthrax in envelopes sent via regular methods in the US Postal service
- Anthrax spores can be spread in the air by missiles, rockets, artillery, aerial bombs and sprayers

---

6. Interview with a DOD official, May 1998 cited in "Former Soviet Biological Weapons Facilities In Kazakhstan: Past, Present, and Future" CNS Occasional Paper available at http://www.cns.miis.edu, accessed on 17 August 2001.
7. Al J. Venter, "Sverdlovsk Outbreak: A Portent of Disaster," *Jane's Intelligence Review*, Vol. 10, No. 5 (May 1998): 36-39; Ian Hoffman, "Piece Found In Anthrax Mystery: Lab Sheds Light on Russian Leak," *Albuquerque Journal*, 3 February, 1998, available at http://www.abqjournal.com/scitech/1sci2-3.htm, accessed on 30 July 2002.
8. From http://www.anthrax.osd.mil/threat/topChoice.asp, accessed on 17 October 2002

- Anthrax can travel downwind for hundreds of miles.
- Anthrax spores can remain active for at least three decades[9]
- Moreover, burrowing rodents such as gophers, field mice, and marmots are natural hosts of plague and other pathogens, and can migrate over long distances spreading infectious disease.
- Naturally occurring anthrax spores remain dormant in the soil for decades. Grazing animals can ingest them and become infected with the disease.
- Anthrax can be produced in large quantities with relatively basic technology.
- Almost all of the technology required to produce anthrax is considered dual-use, meaning that it has legitimate uses in the biological pharmaceutical industries.
- The technology is also available on the open market and has very few controls over the purchaser.
- Any country that has the basic heath care or a basic pharmaceutical industry has the expertise, knowledge and necessary infrastructure to produce anthrax.

Legal aspect: The most worrying aspect now is that a precedent once having been set, it may not be unusual for us to witness another cadre of terrorists using biological and/or chemical weapons to achieve their objectives. The counter measures against such a strike are few at best, and limited in their scope. What is required is vigilance, preemptory action, and harmonising state and interstate activities because these are convergence points which will yield positive results without being a massive drain on a state's resources. At the policy level, more work is needed in completing and implementing international treaties. The convention for the suppression of terrorist bombing needs to be signed, ratified and implemented effectively, although the more important treaties are the CWC and the Verification Protocol of the BTWC. The Organisation for the Prohibition of Chemical Weapons (OPCW) needs to ensure that States implement the legislative and administrative measures to put the CWC work effectively, and that they are comprehensive enough for the state to enforce the convention effectively in its jurisdiction. The Verification Protocol for the BTCW needs to be completed, and the

9. During the Second World War the British experimented with anthrax on Gruinard Island, 40 years later, the island was still uninhabitable—it had to be decontaminated.

demands of industry accommodated. The protocol needs to ensure that each state party implements measures necessary to enforce Article IV, and possibly harmonise current national variations.

Status of Investigation

- At the beginning of the investigation into the anthrax mail attacks the popular perception was that Al Qaeda was to be blamed for these attacks. But with seemingly no definitive leads in the case, law-enforcement officials continued to re-examine all angles. Once that was ruled out then fingers were raised at the Iraqi and Russian BW programmes.
- Although no homegrown US terrorists have ever used anthrax in an attack, many disgruntled elements are said to be obsessed with biological weapons as evidenced by the hundreds of anthrax hoaxes perpetrated by right-wing groups.
- FBI had released an official profile of the suspect, portraying him as a loner with a scientific background, access to laboratory equipment, and some knowledge of the New Jersey region where all the letters had been mailed. The FBI asked members of the public to study the profile carefully and call in with any information - along with offering a $1.25 million reward.
- Investigations point out that the anthrax strain originated within the US Biodefence programme. The strain and properties of the weaponised anthrax is the Ames strain of the bacteria used by the US Army in biological warfare testing. The DNA sequence of the anthrax sent through the US mail in 2001 confirms suspicions that the bacteria originally came from a US military laboratory.
- The data released uses codenames for the reference strains against which the attack strain was compared. But *The New Scientist* revealed that the two reference strains appeared identical to the attack strain most likely originated at the US Army Medical Research Institute for Infectious Diseases at Fort Detrick (USAMRIID), Maryland.
- The availability of the anthrax spores raised questions on the degree of irresponsibility and lack of security at Fort Detrick, Maryland and other facilities. Questions were also raised about the nature of work at Detrick, and secret biodefence projects that push the limits of international prohibition. All through the early 1990s fears about the security at laboratories were being raised about Soviet facilities and Biopreparat.

- Investigators started zeroing in on domestic facilities and domestic subjects, the perpetrator could be a biowarfare personnel out to prove that the US needs to take its job of Biodefence more seriously. In a related development, a Joint Terrorism Task force was set up, an interagency body that specialises in tracking domestic terrorists.
- The Xerox Machine that was used to photocopy the letters that were sent to the Democratic Senators, NBC and NY Post was identified.
- While one line of investigation also posited that the anthrax attacks were linked to the Iraqi biodefence programme; the current stage of investigative research points in the other direction. Iraq was not to be blamed: First, there is the history of UN weapons inspections in Iraq from 1991 to 1998. It is true that Iraq has not fully complied with its disarmament obligations, particularly in the field of biological weapons. However, this failure does not amount to a retained biological weapons capability. Under a very stringent on-site inspection regime, Iraq's biological weapons programmes were dismantled, destroyed or rendered harmless during the course of hundreds of inspections. The major biological weapons production facility—Al Hakum, which was responsible for producing Iraq's anthrax—was blown up with high explosive charges and all its equipment destroyed. Breweries, animal feed factories, vaccine and drug manufacturing facilities, university research laboratories and all hospitals were subject to constant, repeated inspections. Thousands of swabs and samples were taken from buildings and soil throughout Iraq. While it was impossible to verify that all of Iraq's biological capability had been destroyed, the UN never once found evidence that Iraq had either retained biological weapons or associated production equipment, or was continuing work in the field.[10]
- Profile of the likely perpetrator/s: Professor Barbara Hatch Rosenberg, writing for the Federation of American Scientists based on the evidence, has zeroed in on a man who might have worked at the US military laboratory at Fort Detrick, Maryland. He would have been vaccinated and would have access to classified

---

10. Scott Ritter, "Don't blame Saddam for this one", *The Guardian*, 19 October 2001.

information about modifying the spores to make them remain airborne. She added that he had probably made the anthrax himself. "He grew it, probably on a solid medium, and weaponised it at a private location where he had accumulated the equipment and the material."

References

1. The Federal Bureau of Investigation (FBI). http://www.fbi.gov
2. The Centres for Disease Control and Prevention. http// www.bt.cdc.gov
3. The National Medical Disaster System: http://ndms.dhhs.gov/ NDMS/ndms.html
4. Federation of American Scientists: Working Group on Biological and Toxin Weapons
5. http://www.fas.org/bwc/
6. The Association for Infection Control Practitioners. http:// www.apic.org
7. The Johns Hopkins Centre for Civilian Biodefence. http:// www.hopkins-biodefense.org.
8. WHO: Health Aspects of Biological and Chemical Weapons. www.who.int
9. PAHO/WHO: Pan American Health Organisation. http:// www.paho.org
10. Centre for Non-Proliferation Studies www.cns.miis.edu/pubs./ reports/anthrax.htm

Plague Outbreaks in India : Surat and Himachal Pradesh

Animesh Roul

Within a gap of eight years, plague has struck twice in India. The outbreaks caused panic and necessitated an urgent assessment of our public health apparatus vis-a-vis our vulnerability towards infectious diseases. Generally speaking, the resurgence of epidemics and their effects on society demonstrated at least three vital national security issues. They are human mobility (cross-border and intra- border movements), transparency, and tensions between states, (which includes the threat of biological warfare).[1] The re-emergence of plague in India in 1994 (Surat) and in 2002 (Himachal Pradesh) invokes these issues and calls for national and international discourse on disease control. Whether it was caused by intra-state tensions (biological war) or due to a natural phenomenon is still debatable, especially in the case of Surat. However, the plague which ravaged the Diamond City of Surat and scenic hamlets in Shimla affected the economic and political activity in the country, but also posed a serious threat to our national security.

Before discussing the causes, courses and effects of plague outbreaks in India, it would be useful to know the history and aetiology of this dreadful disease.

History of Plague

Often regarded as a curse from God, plague has its place in every religious scripture. For Christians, it was divine punishment, for Muslims, a symbol of self-sacrifice (martyrdom). In the Hindu scripture (Bhagwat Purana), plague was known as Mahamari, the 'great death' which was caused by rats and mentioned with no blind beliefs attached to it.[2] Derived from a Greek word, plaga, meaning a blow or sudden strike, plague has got a

---

1. Laurie Garrett, "The Return of Infectious Disease", *Foreign Affairs*, Vol.75 (1), January/February 1996, p.73.
2. K. Park, *Preventive and Social Medicine* (16th edn.), Jabalpur, Banarasidas Bhanot 2000, p.220.

detailed description including its clinical manifestations in Thucydides' The History of the Peloponnesian War.[3] The history of plague is documented among the Great Pandemics. There are three plague pandemics so far. The world witnessed the first plague pandemic in AD 542 during the reign of Byzantine emperor, Justinian-I, and for almost six decades it caused widespread casualties.[4] The second pandemic struck Europe in the 14th century. The 'Black Death', as it was called, killed almost 25 million people. It is widely believed that the disease spread through the first recorded incident of biological warfare, in the memoirs of the Italian Gabriele de' Mussi. According to this work, soldiers of the Golden Horde (Mongols) catapulted corpses of plague victims into the besieged Genoese trading port of Caffa (now in Ukraine) on the Black Sea.[5] From here the disease spread to Italy, Spain, England, France, and North Africa and soon engulfed Europe. Even after the great pandemic wore out, plague remained endemic among the rodent population, the main vector of this disease. As a result, the disease surfaced sporadically in Asia and Europe throughout the 17th century. The third pandemic was caused by the increasing human mobility and movement of steamships. It started in the later part of the 19th century in China and reached the Indian shores in 1896, and subsequently other major port cities of the world.[6]

---

3. In the wake of the political struggle between Athens and Sparta, plague broke out in its virulent form causing many deaths in Athens. It also caused total disruption of community ties and massive demoralisation in the society. Also, its impact on military and economic strength resulted in undermining civil and religious institutions. For a detailed description, see Mohan Rao, "Plague: The Fourth Horseman", *Economic and Political Weekly*, Vol. XXIX (42), 15 October 1994, pp.2720-2721.
4. See <http://www.globalterrorism101.com/JustiniansPlague.html>
5. Mark Wheelis, "Biological Warfare at the 1346 Siege of Caffa", *Emerging Infectious Disease* (serial online), Vol.8 (9), September 2002<www.cdc.gov/ nciod/EID/Vol8no9/010536.htm>. Also for a critical analysis see, Vincent Derbes, "De Mussis' and the Great Plague of 1348: A Forgotten Episode of Bacteriological Warfare", *Journal of American Medical Association*, Vol. 196 (1), 1966, pp.59-62.
6. India had experienced plague before, in 1612, which primarily affected Agra city. It was in the modern pandemic era that India experienced the plague in its most virulent form along with United States and many south and central Asian countries. See, S.A.Dhanukar and Avijit Hazra, "Return of the Ancient Scourge", *Science Reporter,* Vol.31 (11), November 1994, p.21.

During this modern pandemic, scientists identified and cultured the plague bacillus after thorough investigations and developed a crude vaccine.[7] However, by this time plague had spread around the globe except for Australia and the endemic foci had established itself in rodent populations in almost every continent, irrespective of climatic conditions. Though the pandemic subsided gradually, it was the international regulations on rat control in ports and ships which largely restricted the spread. Though there were no laboratory-confirmed cases of human plague in India after 1968, the disease continued to be present in its wild life. The foci exist in Maharashtra, Himachal Pradesh, Andhra Pradesh and Tamil Nadu.[8]

The Aetiology

What is plague? How are humans susceptible to it? The answers to these questions depict the aetiology of plague. It is a zoonotic disease primarily spread to humans from its natural hosts, rats. The most common carrier is the wild rat (Tatera Indica). But the transmission occurs when there are some disturbances in the environment which facilitates contacts between wild rats and house rats (Rattus rattus) or field rats. It also gets transmitted to rabbits and squirrels and, through rat fleas (Xenopsylla Cheopis and X brasiilensis), infects the humans.[9] There are three principal clinical manifestations of plague: Bubonic, Pneumonic and Septicaemic. Bubonic plague is characterised by the swelling of lymph nodes (buboes), mainly in the groin and less often in the neck and armpits, depending on the site of the flea bite. It cannot spread from person to person, while pneumonic plague involves the lungs and is highly infectious and can spread among humans as the plague bacillus is present in the sputum. The septicaemic plague is very rare and only occurs when the bacilli

---

7. The plague bacillus was first cultured by Alexander Yersin in Hong Kong, thereafter known as *Yersinia pestis* (also, *Pasturella pestis*). But a French scientist while investigating the bubonic plague in Bombay discovered the connection between rat, rat fleas (Xenopsylla Cheipos) and plague bacillus. Later, Waldemmar Haffkine developed the vaccine, also in Bombay.
8. S.A.Dhanukar and Avijit Hazra, "Return of the Ancient Scourge", *Science Reporter, op.cit.,* p.21.
9. This is the most common mode of transmission of *Y.pestis* to humans. Also infection can be caused by infectious body fluids or tissues (both animal and human) and by inhaling infectious droplets. See, "Of Mice and Men", *Down to Earth* (CSE, New Delhi), 31 October 1994, p.8.

invade the blood stream and even death could occur.[10] Among these three types, pneumonic plague is more fatal, and patients who do not receive treatment within 18 hours after the onset of symptoms are unlikely to survive.

Outbreaks in India

India experienced a plague epidemic in 1895-96, which continued for almost two decades, killing approximately ten million people. One estimate even places the period of outbreaks until 1950 and the number of deaths at 12.5 million.[11] However, it is believed that after 1950, due to the emergence of many broad-spectrum antibiotics and disinfectants like DDT and Gamaxine, the spread / transmission of plague was contained. Upto 1993 two separate incidents of plague occurred but could not be confirmed as plague.[12] This period of quiescence (1967-1993) did raise hopes of human plague eradication and, simultaneously, complacency in the health administration. Ironically, the decade following this quiescence witnessed two plague outbreaks : Surat (1994) and in Hatkoti village near Shimla (2002). The former took a heavy toll that shook India's health infrastructure and urban management to the core.

Plague in Surat. In India, empirical studies shows that the plague occurs either in spring or autumn, but at most times is interrupted by the hot Indian summer.[13] The recent outbreaks only confirmed this pattern. In the case of Surat, the disease broke out in the month of September. It is believed that the earthquake in Beed district in 1993 disturbed the territorial equilibrium between wild rats and house rats, which facilitated fleas jumping their hosts. A flood in the river Tapti aggravated this nature-driven development.[14] Besides, the growth in the city skyline and haphazard planning increasing slums and unhygienic conditions, all

---

10. K.Park, *Preventive and Social Medicine, op.cit.*, p.223.
11. Quoted in V. Ramalingaswami, "The Plague Outbreaks in India", *Current Science*, Vol.71, (10), November 1996, p.781.
12. In the early 1980s, there were two suspected outbreaks of plague in areas in the Tamil Nadu / Andhra Pradesh border and in Himachal Pradesh. See, V.K. Ramachandran, "Plague Through the Centuries", *Frontline,* 21 October 1994, p.18.
13. Samuel K. Cohn Jr., "The Black Death: End of Paradigm", *The American Historical Review*, Vol.107 (3), June 2002, p.725.

combined together to cause the epidemic.

In the first week of September, a bubonic plague outbreak occurred in Mamla village in Beed district of Maharashtra. It began with a sudden rat fall and high flea densities in the area.[15] Within a week, despite massive use of disinfectants like DDT and pesticide sprays, the number of patients rose to 183.[16] When the panic-stricken inhabitants fled the area, they carried the disease to other parts of India.[17] Surat came under the grip of plague, in both forms: bubonic and pneumonic. While the official figure put it at 752:44 (infected: killed) ratio by the end of the month, the truth was more alarming.[18] Although Surat remained the epicentre of the plague outbreak, it spread to other parts of the country, primarily due to unrestricted human movement.

The disease was first reported from Ved Road on the night of 19 September 1994. The victim was declared dead on arrival at the Surat Civil Hospital (SCH). Soon another eight people from the slums of Ved Road, Vatagram and Limbayat areas died. All of them had similar symptoms: high fever, cough and blood in the sputum. Reportedly, these were not sudden deaths. Since 13 September people had been dying of a mysterious fever

---

14. *India Disasters Report: Towards A Policy Initiative*, New Delhi, Oxford University Press, 2000, p.291.
15. This evidence though not widely accepted, was sent in initial reports of a probable plague epidemic in the area. See, V.Ramalingaswami, "Resurgence of the Plague", *Science Reporter,* Vol.31 (11), November 1994, p.15.
16. "The Plague: How Serious is it?" *India Today,* 15 October 1994, p.53.
17. Besides Surat other cases were reported from Maharastra(488), Karnataka (46), Uttar Pradesh(10), Madhya Pradesh (4), New Delhi (68) and Gujarat (77). "International Notes Update: Human Plague-India, 1994", *Centre for Disease Control*, 43(41), 21 October 1994, pp 761-762.
18. "The Scourge: The Indian Plague Epidemic of 1994", *Frontline*, 21 October 1994, pp.4-5. The reports varied from one source to other. It varied to a great extent even in official sources. India's leading daily, *The Times of India,* cited one official report that 24 people died, another widely cited official figure was 45, whilist the Chief Secretary of Gujarat reported 17 deaths by the evening of 22 September. Finally the Indian government reported to the World Health Organisation (WHO) that from 26 August to 18 October, 1994, there were 56 deaths (48 in Surat) due to plague. "International Notes Update: Human Plague-India, 1994", *op.cit.,* pp. 761-762. For on line Morbidity and Mortality Report (MMWR) see URL <www.cdc.gov/mmwr/preview/mmrwhtml/00032992.htm>

then called 'Surat fever'.[19]

Investigation and Control

Till 22 September, the mysterious disease was believed to be pneumonia. After 17 people died and many others were infected, it was suspected that Surat was in the grip of pneumonic plague. Soon the National Institute of Communicable Diseases (NICD), New Delhi, swung into action, and worked with international bodies like the World Health Organisation (WHO) and Centre for Disease Control (CDC) to take necessary measures to control the outbreak. The problem of restricting the disease to certain zones proved an uphill task as the panic-stricken people fled to other parts of the country as soon as the news broke out. Though plague is one of the three diseases (besides, cholera and kala-azar) which can be quarantined by international regulations, it is very difficult to identify, check and restrict the movement of patients especially within the country. Even after the Chief Minister of the State and initial investigation by NICD denied that the disease was plague, people ran helter-skelter within the city. The inhabitants of Surat mainly constituted migrant workers from different states. Migrants from Orissa, Maharashtra, West Bengal, Rajasthan and Bihar are crammed into the city making it a 'big transit camp'.[20] Before any restrictions could be imposed, these migrants took to flight (mainly, by road and railways) to their home states and carried the disease with them.

As the disease spread, various investigating agencies worked relentlessly to contain its spread and prevent further complications. NICD, being the nodal agency on communicable diseases, started its investigations right from 2 September after getting information about the suspected bubonic plague in Mamla. After testing four sera samples, NICD confirmed that all of them were positive for plague antibodies. According to a paper presented by the present Director of NICD , a team from NICD was rushed to the affected area.[21] The paper claimed that 'typical epidemiological events like enhanced rodent activity, higher flea indices, rat fall, clinical cases confirming human bubonic plague and serological results, all in

---

19. Rahul Srivastava, "A Plague on This Country", *Down To Earth* (CSE, New Delhi), 31 October 1994, p.6.
20. V.K.Ramachandran, 'Filth and Decay', *Frontline*, 21 October 1994, p.13.

combine confirmed the outbreak in Mamla and its spread to adjoining areas with diminishing intensity'.[22] But in Surat both pneumonic and bubonic plague had occurred, according to the paper. The main findings regarding the genesis of the outbreak in Surat city confirmed that there had been a spillover infection from wild rodents to city or house rats. This was facilitated by the sudden environmental change in the area due to floods in the catchment areas of the Ukai reservoir and subsequent flashflood in Surat city. After the floodwater began receding on 10 September, the movement of people started and the cleaning operation mainly by community members for some days in the flood affected localities. In this process some might have handled or came in contact with dead and infected rodents or animals and developed the disease.[23]

There are two major bodies working on the scene: WHO International Team and NICD, New Delhi. Initially the WHO Team was not satisfied with the prevailing methods of disease investigation in India. In its Executive Report (22 November 1994) the WHO International Team suggested that there were problems with the investigating laboratories in differentiating real cases of plague from other infectious disease with similar symptoms, both epidemiological and clinical.[24] One of the WHO Team members, May C. Chu, microbiologist at the Reference Laboratory for Plague at the Centre for Disease Control and Prevention (CDC), Fort Collins, USA, denied there were any clearly identified Y.pestis culture associated with any specimen obtained from the suspected plague patients.[25] However, further research confirmed the association of Y.pestis with the epidemic at Surat and Beed, and demonstrated that Y.pestis

---

21. A team consisting of an epidemiologist, an entomologist and a microbiologist was sent immediately to investigate the outbreaks. After a village wise study, it concluded that from 26-27 August to 17-18 September there were 63 cases of suspected bubonic plague. The highest reported cases were from Mamla (38). K.K.Dutta, "Plague Outbreaks in India-1994". This paper was presented at the *National Workshop for Developing Surveillance Mechanism for Pathogens with Biological Warfare Potential*, held 18-19 September 2001, at New Delhi.
22. *Ibid.*
23. "Epidemiological Investigation of Pneumonic Plague Outbreak in Surat During 23-25 September 1994 by the National Institute of Communicable Diseases (NICD), Delhi," Appendix B, in Ghanashyam Shah, *Public Health and Urban Development: The Plague in Surat*, New Delhi: Sage, 1997.
24. V. Ramalingaswami, "Plague Outbreaks in India", *op.cit.*, p.781.

isolates obtained from these regions were identified, most likely clonal in origin, and that the pathogen had an enzootic existence in the region.[26]

Plague, Media and the Controversy

Since the outbreak of the disease, there have been conflicting views in professional circles and controversial reporting in the media as well. The questions, which hovered around, were regarding the identity of the causative agent and whether it was a natural outbreak or not.

The Government of India constituted a Technical Advisory Committee (TAC) immediately under the Chairmanship of V. Ramalingaswami on 11 October 1994 with three major terms of references. They were: [27]

- to elucidate factors responsible for the outbreak of plague and its spread,
- to advise on strategies, policies and programmes for the control of plague,
- to recommend steps for prevention of such outbreaks in future.

TAC's investigation drew flak for two reasons: one, the outbreak had subsided and second, fresh samples were not available. It had to continue the investigation with the clinical samples stored in NICD, New Delhi and Surat. The WHO International Team opined that efforts to isolate and identify the microorganism Y.pestis were not successfull. Even six months after the outbreak, the then WHO Director General, Dr. Hiroshi

---

25. *Ibid.*
26 . For a vivid scientific analysis, see, S.K.Panda, et.al, " The 1994 Plague Epidemics of India: Molecular Diagnosis and Characterisation of *Y.pestis* Isolates from Surat and Beed", *Current Science*, Vol. 71(10), 25 November 1996, pp.794-799.
27. "Summary of the Report of Technical Advisory Committee on Plague", Appendix D, in Ghanashyam Shah, *Public Health and Urban Development: The Plague in Surat*, (New Delhi: Sage 1997), p.292. It entrusted the task of isolation and characterisation of Y.pestis from the clinical samples to the Defence Research and Development Establishment (DRDE), Gwalior. Other major institutes and organisations involved in the TAC were AIIMS, NICD, IMTECH, PGIMER, etc.

Nakajima, said that their experts were not able to isolate the microorganism from Beed samples that had confirmed bubonic plague but they could only confirm the presence of plague bacterium from the Surat sample.[28] However, the TAC Report concluded that pneumonic plague was the cause of the deaths.

The findings of the TAC also ran into trouble when one of its members, Kalyan Banerji of the National Institute of Virology (NIV), Pune, did not sign the document due to disagreements. After a gap of five years, in December 1999, an ex-WHO official, Dr. Satnam Singh (former WHO Programme Director) revived the controversy again. According to him 'the disease which killed 47 people in the Surat city in 1994 and caused economic loss worth $600 million was not plague'. He substantiated his argument by mentioning the Report of the American Public Health Association, Manual on Control of Communicable Diseases, (17th Edition). The manual had added 'Surat plague' in its 16th edition, but deleted it in the 17th edition.[29]

Another controversial aspect of the outbreak was, that the Surat plague was not a natural outbreak, and that the causative organism was suspicious. An Indian weekly magazine, *The Week*, published an interesting story regarding this suspicion. Raising the issue of biowarfare, it zeroed in on two possibilities:[30] first, enemy agents could have introduced mutated and cultured germs into Beed and Surat as there was no sign of natural plague (no rat fall before the outbreak); second, someone could have experimented with a newly developed organisms and their vaccines for biological warfare. The story cited various clinical reports and expert opinion, primarily focussed on the activities of the United States and Russia.[31] As time passed, more information regarding the outbreak came out. Such information, which fuelled further suspicions,

---

28. "WHO Still Puzzled Over Surat Epidemic", *The Hindustan Times*, 14 March 1995.
29. "Surat Epidemic, Plagues Again: Now Ex-WHO Official Contests Diagnosis", *The Indian Express*, 19 December 1999. Also, Satnam Singh pointed out that according to the Chairman of the Expert Committee appointed by the Gujarat Government in 1995, N.R.Mehta, most of the evidence did not support the initial suspected diagnosis of pneumonic plague.
30. R. Prasannan, "Germ War", *The Week*, 9 October 1994, p.28.

came from the Centre for Disease Control and Prevention (CDC). It was stated that the Surat strain of the disease was 'unique' and not related to any known variety of the agent, Y.pestis.[32] However, the then defence science adviser and present President of India Dr. A.P.J. Abdul Kalam, investigated the matter. Though the outcome was never made public, some scientists, who thought that the Surat outbreak was an experiment, believed that the aim could have been to study how the government, the scientific community and the people would react in the event of a real biological weapons attack.[33] However, the TAC Report, including that of the NICD, discounted this theory. The tests at various international institutes and tests at DRDE, Gwalior are supposed to have confirmed that the Surat outbreak was plague and a natural outbreak.[34]

Outbreak in Himachal Pradesh. The second case study, plague in Himachal Pradesh in 2002, was not as controversial as its predecessor. But the outbreak did expose some of the inherent lacunae in our civic health system. It was not the first time that this region experienced plague. In September 1982, NICD diagnosed a mystery fever that had gripped the region as bubonic plague, but the matter was suppressed.[35] The scourge

---

31. For a story related to the US involvement, see, R.Prasannan, "American Hand", *The Week*, 16 October 1994. Regarding Russia's role, the Indian Government received information in the first week of July 1995, about a firm called 'Viva' located in Almaty in Kazakstan selling plague microbes. It became hard to rule out the possibility of militants purchasing the organisms from the Kazak company and releasing it in Surat. For a report see, "Were Ultras Responsible for Surat Plague ?", *Hindustan Times*, 9 July 1995.
32. "New Twist to Plague Story", *Tribune* (Chandigarh), 10 July 1995. It was stated that the strain had a chromosome with a curious extra gene. This gene contained a code for the structure of a single RNA molecule.
33. For example, Prof. Indira Nath of AIIMS, believed that it was not surprising for a genetic engineer to introduce an extra gene or genes into the plague microbe. According to her this organism was one that was intensely studied for its biological warfare potential. See, "Scientists Suspect Plague was Engineered", *Hindustan Times* (New Delhi), 7 July 1995.
34. The test reports from the Centre for Disease Control and Prevention, Fort Collins, USA, the Pasteur Institute, Paris and the Stavropol Research Anti-Plague Institute, Russia confirmed the case as a plague outbreak. See, "Surat Deaths: Expert Discounts Theory of Mysterious Disease", *The Hindu* (Madras) 21 June 1995. Also for a detailed scientific analysis see, H.V. Batra, V.Tuteja and G.S.Agrawal, "Isolation and Identification of Yersinia pestis Responsible for the Plague Outbreaks in India, " *Current Science*, Vol.71 (10), 25 November 1996, pp.787-791.

visited the scenic hamlets again on 5 February 2002. This time the disease was somewhat restricted area-wise and virulence. Out of 16 cases, 4 persons died of pneumonic plague.[36] A NICD team visited the epicentre, Rohru-Jubbal belt of Himachal Pradesh, from 14 to 17 February 2002 to investigate the outbreak and provide other technical guidance to the State Government. Surprisingly, it took fourteen days for the NICD to confirm that the disease was plague.[37]

The experts suggested that the cause of the outbreak was contact between infected animals and human beings. Known as 'Sylvatic plague', which exists in nature, it can be transmitted while handling infected animals. The first victim belonged to Hatkoti village in Rohru subdivision. He had reportedly gone to hunt game and fallen ill after eating the flesh in his in laws house in nearby Gallu village. He died on 4th February of a viral disease. Soon, three of his relatives also died in the hospital. The infection travelled with one relative to Banupur, Uttaranchal. Besides these four deaths, 12 other infected persons got medical attention in different hospitals: five at Civil Hospital Rohru, six at the Post Graduate Institute of Medical Education and Research (PGIMER), Chandigarh, and one at the Indira Gandhi Medical College (IGMC), Shimla.

Remarkably, the spread of the disease was contained with the initial efforts of doctors at Rohru Civil Hospital when they launched a screening drive on their own, much before the official confirmation of the epidemic.[38] It is believed that the experience of locals helped in containing the plague before it could turn epidemic. Also, prompt action by the NICD team and the local health administration under its guidance did a good job in restricting the spread. Some of the important measures undertaken were:[39]

---

35. The outbreak was reportedly suppressed because of the Asian Games, which was scheduled at that time in Delhi. The official death count was eight, though one official of NICD puts the toll at 23. See "Germ of A Problem", *India Today*, 4 March 2002.
36. "Final Investigation Report on Pneumonic Plague: Outbreak in Hatkoti Village, Himachal Pradesh", NICD, New Delhi, February 2002.< http://www.nicd.org/ investreports/2002.02.Plague.asp >
37. "Grim Reminder", *Down to Earth* (CSE, New Delhi), Vol.10 (20), 15 March 2002.p.6.
38. Davinder Kumar, "Death Finds a Hill Station", *Outlook*, 4 March 2002, n.16, 18.

- administration of Chemoprophylaxis (using drugs such as doxycycline and tetracycline) to relatives of the patients and to residents of the affected and neighbouring areas, apart from doctors, paramedics and health workers
- fumigation in the affected villages and transport vehicles;
- last but not least, public awareness campaign.

Conclusion

In an interview in 1994, Ashish Kumar Mukerjee, the then Director General of Health Services (DGHS), India said following the plague in Surat that no mechanism existed to combat situations like Surat and the plague took the health department by surprise.[40]

Though India had a plague surveillance unit since 1975, in Bangalore it is moribund. The TAC, in its report pointed out to the need for a national surveillance and response system in India for the control and prevention of infectious disease. In accordance with the recommendation of the TAC, the Government of India set up a National Apical Advisory Committee (NAAC) for national disease surveillance and response[41]. Its establishment was a landmark event in India's struggle against infectious diseases. On the recommendation of NAAC, the National Surveillance Programme for Communicable Diseases (NSPCD) had been launched with the objective to strengthen the disease surveillance system.

However, after the recent plague epidemic in Himachal Pradesh, the World Health Organisation had consciously taken steps to strengthen the surveillance mechanism against plague in India and countries in the endemic regions of South-East Asia.[42] But it seems the worry is still far from over. People are dying of mysterious fevers that go undetected. Dr. R.V. Swami, who was a member of the TAC, and currently is in the Defence

---

39. *Plague in India*, 20 February 2002<www.who.int/disease-outbreak-news/n2002/February/20february2002.html>
40. Read the full text of the interview in *Down to Earth*, 31 October 1994, pp.50-51.
41. For details of NAAC's activities and the National Surveillance Programme For Communicable Diseases (NSPCD), see http://www.nicd.org/ProgramsNICD.asp

Research and Development Organisation (DRDO), New Delhi, has observed that these sporadic and mysterious epidemics point out that India needs a comprehensive disease surveillance and health care system. Whether it is Siliguri fever or Himachal plague; whether a natural outbreak or through biowarfare (or, bio-terrorism for that matter), disease control and prevention must have priority.

42. "WHO to step up surveillance against plague", *The Hindu*, Friday, 28 June 2002.

Seminar Report

IPCS Conference on Biological Weapons: Terrorism Conflicting Political and Economic Interests New Delhi, 9 October 2002

Divya Srivastava

Introduction

Biological Weapons have always elicited a rather limited interest from academics and policy analysts in India. It will not be an exaggeration to state that 99 per cent of the interest generated in Weapons of Mass Destruction has been on nuclear, rather than biological weapons.

The United States had aborted the Review Conference held last November. The Review Conference will reconvene on 11 November 2002, to complete its unfinished agenda. The IPCS convened this conference against this backdrop where several issues relating to biological weapons and verifying compliance of the BTWC were raised.

CWC and BTWC: Lessons from the Verification Process Arpit Rajain

Discussion

- The worst can happen during a BTWC attack. The time for detection will be protracted and tedious. 9/11 may happen only once but there is a need to be prepared to confront a radiological threat.
- Iraq has acquired the status of a regional power vis-à-vis the nuclear weapon, and Saddam Hussein is aware of the manoeuvrings required to foil the verification protocol.
- There is some ambiguity about the future of the BTWC Protocol after 9/11. The UN is slated to become more irrelevant, with no countervailing force to the US.
- The developing countries feel a sense of futility in joining the Convention. There is not a single arms control treaty that can be

labeled perfect. North Korea was not consistent in adhering by the Non Proliferation Treaty.

- It was agreed that the Westphalian notion of nation states constituting the world order is a prudent one, and applies to the current scenario. A point that elicited consensus was that a verification process is better than none at all. A Convention would at least create a sense of political commitment, and embarrassment for the violator; a norm for compliance is created if there is a verification procedure.
- No Challenge Inspections under the CWC has occurred so far.
- The Ad Hoc Group and the Protocol are dead and an unfinished body of work. The US position has ensured that the work done only remains a historical record.
- The fate of the Ad Hoc Group is sealed; breathing life into it again this year would be difficult. India has an open mind on this issue, which is reflected by the opinions and viewpoints offered by analysts and bureaucrats.
- The international system is a society. The members of this society have to abide by certain rules, independent of their other concerns. It is in the interest of states to continue to cooperate in an anarchic world order.

BTWC State Implementation: National Legislation to Deal with the Situation – Can They Substitute the Protocol?
G. Balachandran

Discussion

- It is important to have a system of control within the Convention processes and not have the technology controlled by a group of countries. The developing countries should aim at having an international Convention, and influence that body on the measures to be acted upon.
- Biotechnology is in the same condition today as electronics before the invention of the transistor. The field will be witnessing tremendous growth.
- National Implementation procedures are invaluable for any country in the world when the threat from biological and chemical weapons is serious.

- National Implementation measures provide additional security to a state. Even though they might appear tedious and time-consuming, they will be worth the while.
- A Protocol would help, as it has two benefits. Firstly, non-compliance becomes awkward, causes embarrassment, and would be avoided by countries. The world can come together to devise an end to this kind of weaponry.
- The US superiority and its smugness need to be countered. The world has to start working towards establishing a Protocol at the global level.
- The elements that are a must for implementation are an extradition clause. A strong regulatory mechanism is also extremely important. It took Bangladesh 12-13 years of coaxing Pakistan to establish an extradition treaty..
- A Convention which lacks even the basic verification measures will lead to problems, sooner or later. If there is no Protocol, no voluntary control over technology transfers will take place.
- For every advance in defensive technology, there is a significant rise in offensive technology.
- The countries should begin to work diligently towards national implementation measures.

Compulsions of the Biotech Industry/ Reservations Regarding the BTWC Protocol and Suggested Solutions Sandhya Tiwari and Divya Chopra

Discussion

- India did not get a World Health Organisation (WHO) certification for manufacturing and exporting state-of-the-art biological agents. There has to be a suitable regulatory system in place, and industry must not be subjected to ad hoc certification procedures.
- Also, multiple agencies are involved in administering this process. This only leads to chaos and a regime which lacks clear direction.
- In the 1980s, research in biotechnology was confined to laboratories. The last five years have witnessed tremendous growth. For instance, seventy biotech companies were launched in the last four years.

- The position of the United States vis-à-vis Indian industry has changed after 11 September. The way the Protocol was viewed prior to 11 September and the manner in which companies came under the purview of declarations witnessed a transformation. It was agreed earlier that small vaccine manufacturing units should be outside the purview of declarations.
- The area of biotechnology is very complex, as this regime is dominated by patents. It is not a single technology sector.
- A strong legislation for technology transfer is essential.
- The industry has been extremely cooperative with the government in regard to the suspicious outbreak of diseases, essentially because the government has taken the industry along.
- The key is to maintain a balance between the Protocol's prohibitions and its verification process. Misuse of the verification process could be debilitating.
- An issue that elicited consensus was that the system for ensuring biosafety, is not adequate and requires attention.
- There is need for a strong regulatory mechanism to be adopted and effectively implemented.

Endgame in November 2002: US Position – Other Alternative Modalities to Protocol
Kalpana Chittaranjan

Discussion

- The World Health Organisation (WHO) is currently evaluating suspicious outbreaks of diseases.
- It is difficult to ascertain exactly what it is that the Americans desire out of the BW Convention and believe about its future.
- The Americans do not want a Verification Protocol. Academics and analysts across the board might be divided on this. There are biodefense measures proceeding in the US that might not be consistent with their obligations under the BTWC. The US appears divided into two schools of thought. One school advocates that the US does not want a multilateral Protocol, as it has candidly displayed its proclivity towards unilateral action. But, when the US needs cooperation from the international community for its own purpose, it justifies this as a 'global cause'. It is almost a raw

exercise of political power.

- A drawback of the Protocol is that it focuses very narrowly upon the requirements of developed countries, which possess sophisticated, advanced weapons.
- There is a lesson to be learnt from the SALT (Strategic Arms Limitation Talks) agreement. A verification mechanism is imperative and needs to be driven by considerations, or else, these issues could become severely politicised, leading to problems.
- It is possible to motivate religious fundamentalists, like the *fidayeen.* After all, there was a guiding principle motivating the people who undertook the 9/11 attacks.

India's Position on the BTWC and its Verification Protocol
P. R. Chari and Arpit Rajain

Discussion

- The stance adopted by this paper differs from the official views of the Government of India.
- The BWC Convention was born out of the womb of the Cold War. Since then, India has been consistent about supporting disarmament. India was actively involved in the discussions on the BWC. India's perception of International Relations at that point was shaped by its disarmament and NAM driven policies.
- The Biological Weapons Convention (1972) was signed after an assessment of its virtues and shortcomings. The treaty had certain verification problems, but the superpowers were unwilling to get involved in their detailed investigation. India made several efforts in the direction of disarmament. Through the six-nation initiative in the 1980s, India hoped that the world would eventually inch towards nuclear elimination.
- The happenings before 9/11 are independent of what happened subsequently. Post 11 September, a great deal of emphasis had been placed on fighting bio-terrorism. Prior to 9/11, it was unthinkable that non-state actors could use bio weapons with effortless ease to wreak havoc on human beings. Post 9/11, non-state actors entered the scene. In these newly emerged circumstances, India has been seeking to strengthen the Protocol.
- The fate of the upcoming Review Conference is sealed. It had an

agenda last year, and will resume negotiations on that agenda. But the possibility of instilling life into the process remains a moot question. It appears that the Americans will have to explore other options. India had displayed eagerness to finalise the Verification Protocol. Of course, what emerges in its place will depend upon consultations between the State Parties, but the situation is difficult. The picture that emerges is somewhat grey.

- The prognosis for the upcoming Conference does not appear healthy and positive, but there is always the possibility of a miracle.
- The US went in for the BTWC with the full consciousness that the Convention was basically 'unverifiable', since a fool-proof verification of BTWC activities was practically impossible.
- It was agreed that between the years 1972 and 1985, biotechnology took off in a big way. Non-verification left a loophole for mutual accusations.
- Biological Weapons and bio warfare could become the weapons of choice for non-state actors, but verification continues to be difficult.
- Going ahead without the United States backing the Protocol would be unrealistic. 'Who will listen to you?' was the nagging query raised about going ahead with the Convention without the United States.
- India is fully aware that Pakistan possesses Chemical Weapons whilst masquerading as a non-possessor.
- The next step in international relations is to ensure that prohibition regimes are made more effective.

Threat Analysis of Danger from Bioweapons and Biodefence Measures

Major General Ashok Krishna, AVSM (Retd)

Discussion

- The United States, without doubt, is largely ahead of other nations in technological advancement. While the United States created a furore about Iraq possessing chemical weapons during the Gulf War (1991), and used the international coalition to weaken the Iraqi economy and the country, the quantities of chemical and biological weapons the US possesses is not known. This is sheer hypocrisy and the international community needs to stand up against it.

- There is no doubt that Saddam Hussein's administration is bent on taking on the US and its allies. Their investment in the development of nuclear, biological, and chemical weapons has been continuous.
- Some facts regarding Iraq's nuclear weaponry have been quoted by a recent CIA study. Who will muster the gumption or audacity to ask the Americans for verification of its own weapons?
- An enemy like Iraq can never be trusted and should not be diplomatically isolated. Or else, it would cause problems for the international community. After 1998, there have been no inspections. The nations of the world must unite on the agenda to cripple its nuclear programme.
- Biological weapons can be best used in the form of aerosols; to disperse them effectively is the main problem.
- Biological weapons cannot be directly delivered, as aerosolisation is difficult.
- The best way to disperse biological weapons is by rockets.

BW Terrorism: History, Nature, Likelihood, Countermeasures
PR Chari

Discussion

- It is easier to manufacture a chemical weapon than a biological one. Biological weapons require a higher level of sophistication and knowledge, but have greater versatility.
- There is a fear of nation states making use and, on several occasions having used, biological weapons while engaged in armed conflict. The Americans have displayed great concern. Americans are spread across the globe; 65,000 in India alone. So, if the weapons are used, a significant number of Americans could get affected.
- There is a growing concern about non-state actors getting access to biological weapons.
- There is a great need to psychologically profile the terrorist. It is

important to comprehend the phenomenon of religious terrorism, whereby an individual is willing to sacrifice himself for a cause, which rational thinking does not allow room for.

- According to religious terrorists, biological warfare is a plague, and some religions consider plague as divine punishment.
- It is not prudent to group biological weapons with Weapons of Mass Destruction (WMD). Anthrax mail attacks and the Tokyo subway attack do not qualify these weapons to be classified as WMD.
- International cooperation is required to fight biological warfare and religious terrorism, but will be difficult to garner.

Plague Outbreaks in India: Surat and Himachal Pradesh Animesh Roul

Discussion

- The National Institute of Communicable Diseases, NICD, took fourteen days to confirm the Himachal epidemic as plague. It is vital that the Ministry of Public Health realizes the huge responsibility that it shoulders. It should invest more to provide adequate security for the nation's population and upgrade the equipment and machinery for diagnosis. Under no circumstance can it be allowed to take 14 days to diagnose a disease as diabolical as plague. This period must be reduced.
- The government needs to provide appropriate mechanisms. Surveillance in India is practically defunct. The means and system of surveillance need to be in sound shape.
- There is an alarming lack of accountability among the officials concerned, particularly when accidents occur. The information management system, coupled with a disaster management system, need to be coordinated.
- Plague holds a great potential for serious consequences. Therefore, it is absolutely imperative to improve the health machinery.

The Anthrax Scare
Vivek Shankar Mathur and Arpit Rajain

Discussion

- There is an immediate need to adopt and implement effective steps to tackle the threat from this new threat from anthrax.
- The investigation in the US, still ongoing, reveals that the perpetrator(s) are/were the biowarfare or biodefence personnel, out to prove that the US needs to take its biodefence more seriously. The pattern of investigation reveals that it is imperative that the US turns the searchlight inwards within the domestic arena and does not blame Al Qaeda or Iraq for everything.
- Anthrax does not qualify for use as a WMD. It can be used as a deadly weapon only at the individual level, not as a weapon of mass destruction.
- Though access to raw materials required for manufacturing anthrax spores is easy to obtain, its weaponisation is difficult. It is a double-edged weapon, but to make it a potent bioweapon requires a good deal of scientific knowledge.

APPENDIX

The Biological and Toxin Weapons Convention[1]

Convention on the Prohibition of the Development, Production and Stockpiling of Bacteriological (Biological) and Toxin Weapons and on Their Destruction

Signed at London, Moscow and Washington on 10 April 1972.
Entered into force on 26 March 1975
Depositaries: UK, US and Soviet governments.

The States Parties to this Convention,

Determined to act with a view to achieving effective progress towards general and complete disarmament, including the prohibition and elimination of all types of weapons of mass destruction, and convinced that the prohibition of the development, production and stockpiling of chemical and bacteriological (biological) weapons and their elimination, through effective measures, will facilitate the achievement of general and complete disarmament under strict and effective international control,

Recognising the important significance of the Protocol for the Prohibition of the Use in War of Asphyxiating, Poisonous or Other Gases, and of Bacteriological Methods of Warfare, signed at Geneva on 17 June 1925, and conscious also of the contribution which the said Protocol has already made, and continues to make, to mitigating the horrors of war,

Reaffirming their adherence to the principles and objectives of that Protocol and calling upon all States to comply strictly with them,

Recalling that the General Assembly of the United Nations has repeatedly condemned all actions contrary to the principles and objectives of the Geneva Protocol of 17 June 1925,

---

1 Available at http://projects.sipri.se/cbw/docs/bw-btwc-text.html, accessed on 25 November 2002

Desiring to contribute to the strengthening of confidence between peoples and the general improvement of the international atmosphere, Desiring also to contribute to the realisation of the purposes and principles of the United Nations,

Convinced of the importance and urgency of eliminating from the arsenals of States, through effective measures, such dangerous weapons of mass destruction as those using chemical or bacteriological (biological) agents, Recognising that an agreement on the prohibition of bacteriological (biological) and toxin weapons represents a first possible step towards the achievement of agreement on effective measures also for the prohibition of the development, production and stockpiling of chemical weapons, and determined to continue negotiations to that end,

Determined for the sake of all mankind, to exclude completely the possibility of bacteriological (biological) agents and toxins being used as weapons,

Convinced that such use would be repugnant to the conscience of mankind and that no effort should be spared to minimise this risk,

Have agreed as follows:

Article I

Each State Party to this Convention undertakes never in any circumstances to develop, produce, stockpile or otherwise acquire or retain:

(1) Microbial or other biological agents, or toxins whatever their origin or method of production, of types and in quantities that have no justification for prophylactic, protective or other peaceful purposes;

(2) Weapons, equipment or means of delivery designed to use such agents or toxins for hostile purposes or in armed conflict.

Article II

Each State Party to this Convention undertakes to destroy, or to divert to peaceful purposes, as soon as possible but not later than nine months after entry into force of the Convention, all agents, toxins, weapons, equipment and means of delivery specified in Article I of the Convention, which are in its possession or under its jurisdiction or control. In implementing the provisions of this article all necessary safety precautions shall be observed to protect populations and the environment.

Article III

Each State Party to this Convention undertakes not to transfer to any recipient whatsoever, directly or indirectly, and not in any way to assist, encourage, or induce any State, group of States or international organisations to manufacture or otherwise acquire any of the agents, toxins, weapons, equipment or means of delivery specified in Article I of this Convention.

Article IV

Each State Party to this Convention shall, in accordance with its constitutional processes, take any necessary measures to prohibit and prevent the development, production, stockpiling, acquisition, or retention of the agents, toxins, weapons, equipment and means of delivery specified in Article I of the Convention, within the territory of such State, under its jurisdiction or under its control anywhere.

Article V

The States Parties to this Convention undertake to consult one another and to cooperate in solving any problems which may arise in relation to the objective of, or in the application of the provisions of, the Convention. Consultation and Cooperation pursuant to this article may also be undertaken through appropriate international procedures within the framework of the United Nations and in accordance with its Charter.

Article VI

(1) Any State Party to this convention which finds that any other State Party is acting in breach of obligations deriving from the provisions of the Convention may lodge a complaint with the Security Council of the

United Nations. Such a complaint should include all possible evidence confirming its validity, as well as a request for its consideration by the Security Council.

(2) Each State Party to this Convention undertakes to cooperate in carrying out any investigation which the Security Council may initiate, in accordance with the provisions of the Charter of the United Nations, on the basis of the complaint received by the Council. The Security Council shall inform the States Parties to the Convention of the results of the investigation.

Article VII

Each State Party to this Convention undertakes to provide or support assistance, in accordance with the United Nations Charter, to any Party to the Convention which so requests, if the Security Council decides that such Party has been exposed to danger as a result of violation of the Convention.

Article VIII

Nothing in this Convention shall be interpreted as in any way limiting or detracting from the obligations assumed by any State under the Protocol for the Prohibition of the Use in War of Asphyxiating, Poisonous or Other Gases, and of Bacteriological Methods of Warfare, signed at Geneva on 17 June 1925.

Article IX

Each State Party to this Convention affirms the recognised objective of effective prohibition of chemical weapons and, to this end, undertakes to continue negotiations in good faith with a view to reaching early agreement on effective measures for the prohibition of their development, production and stockpiling and for their destruction, and on appropriate measures concerning equipment and means of delivery specifically designed for the production or use of chemical agents for weapons purposes.

Article X

(1) The States Parties to this Convention undertake to facilitate, and have the right to participate in, the fullest possible exchange of equipment, materials and scientific and technological information for the use of bacteriological (biological) agents and toxins for peaceful purposes. Parties to the Convention in a position to do so shall also cooperate in contributing individually or together with other States or international organisations to the further development and application of scientific discoveries in the field of bacteriology (biology) for prevention of disease, or for other peaceful purposes.

(2) This Convention shall be implemented in a manner designed to avoid hampering the economic or technological development of States Parties to the Convention or international cooperation in the field of peaceful bacteriological (biological) activities, including the international exchange of bacteriological (biological) and toxins and equipment for the processing, use or production of bacteriological (biological) agents and toxins for peaceful purposes in accordance with the provisions of the Convention.

Article XI

Any State Party may propose amendments to this Convention. Amendments shall enter into force for each State Party accepting the amendments upon their acceptance by a majority of the States Parties to the Convention and thereafter for each remaining State Party on the date of acceptance by it.

Article XII

Five years after the entry into force of this Convention, or earlier if it is requested by a majority of Parties to the Convention by submitting a proposal to this effect to the Depositary Governments, a conference of States Parties to the Convention shall be held at Geneva, Switzerland, to review the operation of the Convention, with a view to assuring that the purposes of the preamble and the provisions of the Convention, including the provisions concerning negotiations on chemical weapons, are being realised. Such review shall take into account any new scientific and technological developments relevant to the Convention.

Article XIII

(1) This Convention shall be of unlimited duration.
(2) Each State Party to this Convention shall in exercising its national sovereignty have the right to withdraw from the Convention if it decides that extraordinary events, related to the subject matter of the Convention, have jeopardised the supreme interests of its country. It shall give notice of such withdrawal to all other States Parties to the Convention and to the United Nations Security Council three months in advance. Such notice shall include a statement of the extraordinary events it regards as having jeopardised its supreme interests.

Article XIV

(1) This Convention shall be open to all States for signature. Any State which does not sign the Convention before its entry into force in accordance with paragraph (3) of this Article may accede to it at any time.

(2) This Convention shall be subject to ratification by signatory States. Instruments of ratification and instruments of accession shall be deposited with the Governments of the United States of America, the United Kingdom of Great Britain and Northern Ireland and the Union of Soviet Socialist Republics, which are hereby designated the Depositary Governments.

(3) This Convention shall enter into force after the deposit of instruments of ratification by twenty-two Governments, including the Governments designated as Depositaries of the Convention.

(4) For States whose instruments of ratification or accession are deposited subsequent to the entry into force of this Convention, it shall enter into force on the date of the deposit of their instruments of ratification or accession.

(5) The Depositary Governments shall promptly inform all signatory and acceding States of the date of each signature, the date of deposit or each instrument of ratification or of accession and the date of entry into force of this Convention, and of the receipt of other notices.

(6) This Convention shall be registered by the Depositary Governments pursuant to Article 102 of the Charter of the United Nations.

Article XV

This Convention, the English, Russian, French, Spanish and Chinese texts of which are equally authentic, shall be deposited in the archives of the Depositary Governments. Duly certified copies of the Convention shall be transmitted by the Depositary Governments to the Governments of the signatory and acceding states.

CONTRIBUTORS

P. R. Chari is a former member of the Indian Administrative Service. During the course of his official career, he served two spells (1971-75 and 1985-88) in the Ministry of Defence. His last position there was Additional Secretary. He was Director of the Institute for Defence Studies and Analyses. New Delhi (1975-80), International Fellow, Centre for International Affairs, Harvard University (1983-84), and Research Professor, Centre for Policy Research (1992-96). Currently he is Director of the Institute of Peace and Conflict Studies, New Delhi. He has worked extensively on nuclear disarmament, non-proliferation and Indian defence issues. He has published over 1100op-ed articles in newspapers/websites and over 100 monographs and major papers in learned journals/chapters in books in India and abroad.

His books include:

Indo-Pak Nuclear Stand Off: Role of the United States (1995);
Co-author, *Brasstacks and Beyond: Perception and Management Crisis* (1995)
Co-author and Co-editor, *Nuclear Non-Proliferation in India and Pakistan: South Asian Perspectives* (1996);
Editor, *India: Towards Millennium* (1998);
Editor, *Perspectives on National Security in South Asia: In Search of a New Paradigm (1999)*
Co-editor, *Kargil: The Tables Turned* (2001)
Co-author, *The Simla Agreement,* 1972 (2001)
Editor, *Security and Governance in South Asia* (2001)
Co-editor, *Working Towards a Verification Protocol for Biological Weapons (2001)*

Currently he has under publication co-authored book on the Spring 1990 Crisis in Indo-Pak Relations (Routledge UK), Co-editor, Human Security in South Aisa (2003). He is also working on edited volumes on *Nuclear Stability in South Asia, Energy Security in India.*

Arpit Rajain has been working as Research Officer in the Institute of Peace and Conflict Studies since 1997 on WMD issues. Under a grant from the Ministry of External Affairs, Government of India, he co-edited (with Mr. P. R. Chari) *Working Towards a Verification Protocol for Biological* Weapons (New Delhi: IPCS, 2001). He has published several research papers in reputed journals and articles in newspapers/websites. He has presented papers at various forums including Cambridge University, Harvard University, Indiana University, the University of California at San Diego, APCSS (Hawaii), ISODARCO (Italy) and the Wilton Park (UK) on South Asian security and WMD issues. He has actively participated in Pugwash Working Groups on WMD. Currently he is working on a monograph *Deterring Nuclear Conflict in Southern Asia*, an edited volume *Nuclear Stability in South Asia* and his doctoral thesis, "Negotiating the Biological Weapons Convention" at the Centre for International Politics, Organisation and Disarmament in the School of International Studies, JNU, New Delhi. His research interests include WMD proliferation and terrorism, Indian Foreign Policy and disarmament issues.

Dr. G. Balachandran is an independent economist/ analyst specialisng in country risk analysis, security issues and industry and trade issues. He was the Director of the India centre of a multicountry UNDP project, TIPS, which set up and ran a trade promotion computer-linked trade information network in the late 1980s. He was a Senior Visiting Scientist at the Carnegie Mellon University in the early 1990s. His other stints have included: the development Correspondent of the Hindu; consultant in S&T to the Brazilian Embassy in India; consulting editor, *The Business Standard,* etc. He specialises in security studies, psephology and global economy principally country risk analysis.

Dr. Sandhya Tewari heads the biotechnology desk at Confederation of Indian Industry (CII), which is the foremost industry association in India with a direct membership of over 4,000 companies. A facilitator, CII catalyses change by working closely with the government on policy issues, enhancing efficiency, competitiveness and expanding business opportunities for industry through a range of specialised services and global linkages. Sandhya has been spearheading the biotechnology initiative of CII for the last 5 years. Her work involves promotion of Indian industry in this sector through close interaction with the government on policy issues and creating awareness of new opportunities. she began her career as a scientist working for Ranbaxy. She also worked briefly as a lecturer, teaching a post graduate biotech course before joining

CII. She holds a Ph.D. in Plant Molecular Biology from the University of Manitoba in Winnipeg, Canada.

Divya Chopra has recently joined the Biotechnology and Pharmaceuticals Division of the holds an MSc degree in Organisational and Social Psychology from the London School of Economics and Political Science, United Kingdom. Her main areas of interest are Individual Organisational Change, Organisational and Industrial Restructuring, and Research and Publication, with a specific focus on Health Care and Social Issues.

Maj Gen Ashok Krishna, AVSM, was commissioned into the Indian Army in 1957. He has held various staff appointments including in Military Operations Directorate and the Army Headquarters. He was Commander, Higher Command Wing, College of Combat Mhow at the time of his retirement in 1994. He has written several articles on insurgency and terrorism, has authored *India's Armed Forces: Fifty Years of War and Peace*, and co-edited *Kargil: The Tables Turned*. His areas of interest include insurgency, terrorism and Kashmir.

Dr. Kalpana Chittaranjan is presently a Research Officer at the Institute for Defence Studies and Analyses, New Delhi. She has been writing on non-proliferation issues (nuclear and biological arms control) for over a decade. Her publications include " History of the BTWC and AHG" in P. R. Chari and Arpit Rajain (eds.), *Working Towards a Verification Protocol for Biological Weapons*, New Delhi: IPCS, 2001). Her articles have been published in leading research journals (like 'Strategic Analysis') and newspapers (like *The Hindu* and *The Times of India).*

Vivek Shankar Mathur has a Masters Degree in Politics and specialised in International Relations from the School of International Studies, Jawaharlal Nehru University, New Delhi. His areas of interest include WMD Non-Proliferation, and Globalisation and Interdependence in Communications Security.

Animesh Roul is currently working as a Research Associate at the Institute for Conflict Management, New Delhi. A Doctoral candidate at the Centre for International Politics, Organisation and Disarmament, School of International Studies, JNU, New Delhi. Dissertation at M.Phil level: "The Environmental Effects of the Production and Use of Weapons of Mass Destruction (NBC)". Interest areas: Armed forces, WMD proliferation, terrorism and environmental issues. His publications include "The BWC: Current Status of Negotiation and Position of Member States", in P. R. Chari and Arpit Rajain (eds.), *Working Towards a Verification Protocol for Biological Weapons* (New Delhi: IPCS, 2001); "Mass Destruction At The Door Step", *Down To Earth*, CSE, New Delhi, Vol.10 (12), 15 November 2001; "Biological Weapon: Most Preferred WMD", in the website of Institute for Peace and Conflict Studies, New Delhi, and "Back to Beginning: Afghanistan", *Down To Earth*, Centre for Science and Environment , 31 May 2002.

Divya Srivastava completed her major in English literature from St. Xavier's Mumbai and went to the London School of Economics to pursue a Masters degree in International Relations. Her research interests include Weapons of Mass Destruction, security concerns in Southeast Asia and Indo-US security relations.

INDEX

About India Research Press

India Research Press is a collectively run book publisher with support of Authors and Editors. Since our founding in 1999, we have tried to meet the needs of readers who are exploring, or are committed to the politics of change.

Our goal is to publish books that encourage critical thinking and constructive action on the key political, cultural, social, economic and ecological issues shaping life in the Indian Sub-continent and in the world. In this way, we hope to give expression to a wide diversity of democratic and social movements.

India Research Press publishes Original works-as well as-works under Rights with various University and Academic publishers throughout the world.

Since our conception, we have added two new imprints to our existing line of Academic publishing.The Group now has three seperate divisions & editors for its publishing programme and many new titles, scheduled in the coming months. The India Research Press also has New Overseas Distributors for the sale of its titles in the USA and the European continent. The group is proud to introduce its three divisions of publishing.

India Research Press **Academic Publishing Division.**

TARA press **General Division – Mass Market including Fiction.**

Swankit **General Division – Health, Non Fiction and Educational titles.**

The group is headed by Anuj Bahri Malhotra, its CEO & Commissioning Manager. He is assisted by an efficient and professional staff of Editors, Administrator, Office Assistants and Accountant. Born to a bookseller's family, running the most sought after bookshop [Bahri Sons] in the country, Anuj has a long 23 years experience in the Indian Book Industry.